Rejoice
Always

Dr. Michael Shapiro
&
Dr. Mary Shapiro

Rejoice
Always

A Handbook for Disciples Facing
Emotional Challenges

DPI

DISCIPLESHIP
PUBLICATIONS
INTERNATIONAL

To the original members of the
Rejoice Always group,
who taught us about faithful perseverance
in the face of emotional challenges

Contents

Acknowledgments

The opportunity to author a book is truly the fulfillment of a lifelong dream for Mary and me. To be able to do so while serving God's kingdom is no less than an honor. To this end, we are very grateful to the ministry leaders and elders of the Atlanta and Athens regions of the International Churches of Christ for their open-mindedness regarding the subject of this book. The idea that true Christians who live a godly life can still suffer from psychiatric illnesses is not accepted by everyone. Therefore, we would like to thank Steve and Kim Sapp, as well as Sonny and Carolyn Sessions, for being sensitive to the need to address mental health problems in God's church. We would also like to thank Don and Lee Burroughs for supporting us wholeheartedly when we came up with the idea for the Rejoice Always group, which eventually became the impetus for this book.

We owe our lives to our parents, who have loved us unconditionally and have always provided us with every opportunity for success. We owe our souls to our "spiritual parents" and very best friends, Greg and Kay Garcia, who led us to Christ in the first place.

We would also like to thank our children, Amanda, Robbie, and Emily, for enduring more than a few frozen pizzas while we struggled to get this book done "after hours."

Thanks are also due to Tom Jones and his staff at DPI, who have been a joy to work with and have patiently nursed us through our first (but hopefully not last) major writing project.

Most of all, we are grateful to God, whose ways are as high above ours as the heavens are above the earth (Isaiah 55: 8-9) and whose paths are beyond tracing out (Romans 11: 33). Only he truly knows the mind and emotions of man.

Foreword

How long will you hide your face from me?
　How long must I wrestle with my thoughts
and every day have sorrow in my heart?
　How long will my enemy triumph over me?

Psalm 13:1-2

More than fifteen years ago, I read this psalm while sitting by a lake in northern Missouri. As I thought about the struggle David described, I penned my own lament. "Father," I wrote, "I would have never dreamed that one who has been seeking you for as long as I have could possibly feel this bad." For weeks my emotions had been at the very bottom. For days on end my thoughts had tormented me, accused me and left me feeling that there just might be no hope. I had made an important decision to lead a new church planting and now, given my emotional state, that idea seemed preposterous. I had relatively good health, was the husband of a wonderful woman and the father of three beautiful children—and most of all, had a great purpose in life. But I felt that I wanted to die. As I look back on it now, it is obvious that I was deeply and clinically depressed and remained that way for some time to come. I counted among my friends some outstanding spiritual leaders, but they were just as unprepared to deal with my depression as I was. No one knew quite what to say or what to do. However, by the grace of God, I had an amazing wife and faithful friends, who loved me unconditionally and believed in me, even when I felt with the writer of Psalm 88 that "the darkness is my closest friend."

Surrounded by such *agape* love, I eventually began to learn to live again in spite of this oppressor that Churchill referred to as "the black dog." Over time, I learned some powerful lessons about how a Christian can still rejoice even when perplexed and besieged by emotional challenges. I came to see that God can still work amazingly even with this kind of weakness, which can seem so debilitating. I finally, and quite remarkably, arrived at a point where I could laugh at depression and taunt it as Paul does death in 1 Corinthians 15:55. I could say, "Depression, you seem so dominant, but thanks be to God, you will not have the victory." I am prone to depression and probably will be until I die. (The fact that I have multiple sclerosis may contribute to that.) But I have learned that depression does not have to have the last word—not when we serve the God who overcomes.

Because of my own experience and because of my desire to see disciples who suffer from various emotional challenges receive the help they need, I am grateful that God has prepared Doctors Michael and Mary Shapiro both professionally and spiritually to address the issues you will find in this book. Many disciples who already face emotional or psychiatric challenges carry the added burden of unnecessary guilt over their condition. They suffer first from the condition itself and then additionally from all kinds of misunderstanding. The Shapiros do not encourage anyone with emotional problems to see themselves as victims, nor do they encourage friends or spiritual leaders to see them that way, but their insights will shed much-needed light on a subject we have not adequately addressed as a movement.

Prayerfully, this book will help both those who are emotionally challenged and those who help them to have a more accurate understanding of these challenges and then to find God's answers which truly enable us all to be overcomers.

Thomas Jones
Boston, Massachusetts

Why This Book Had to Be Written

> Rejoice in the Lord always. I will say it again: Rejoice!
>
> Philippians 4:4

To some disciples, the scripture above represents an impossible command. They can go to church, reach out to others and even be fruitful in various ways, but feeling happy enough to rejoice seems completely out of their grasp.

As psychologists who are also Christians, we have seen many brothers and sisters like this in our office through the years. They have called us or visited us from all over the country, because disciples are much more comfortable discussing their "emotional problems" with fellow Christians than with mental health professionals in the world.

It has occurred to us that the questions and quandaries faced by disciples with psychiatric or emotional problems are similar from place to place, person to person. Most often, disciples are trying to learn how to define (or erase) the fine line between their faith and their emotional difficulties. We have dealt with the same issues so many times that we have come to see the need to educate and inform disciples en masse.

For a time we tried to lead a support group for Christians with psychiatric problems, dubbed the "Rejoice Always" group, but it quickly became overfilled with brothers and sisters who would come every week from as far away as adjoining states!

So, the time has come for us to write a book. Our intention is to inform Christians who have a history of psychiatric problems, as well as their fellow Christians who are called upon to help them. This book should also prove helpful to ministry leaders who lack a fundamental knowledge of psychiatric disorders and are therefore ill prepared to counsel Christians who are suffering in this way.

The specific purpose of this work is to help the reader understand how psychiatric disorders challenge and affect a Christian's faith. Hopefully, the reader will come to conclude that regardless of any psychiatric condition, a committed Christian can still glorify God and has no less of a responsibility to please God, serve others and save the lost. We also hope that this book will help Christians with emotional problems see that their struggles are not as uncommon as they think, and as a result, they will be encouraged to discuss their struggles openly and to seek treatment if necessary.

Most of all, our ultimate goal will have been met if the information in this book helps even one Christian to overcome and remain faithful to God despite a psychiatric or emotional challenge.

1

The Big Question: How Much Is Sin, and How Much Is Psychological?

It never fails. We see them time and again in our practice—disciples with chronic or longstanding emotional problems who had expected their problems to disappear at their baptism. They appear at our office reluctantly, usually on the insistence of their spouse or discipling partner. Stiff-lipped and frustrated, they offer their litany of symptoms and problems. However, goodhearted disciples that they are, they are quick to attribute their problems to either sin or lack of commitment. Since their problems involve feelings and emotions, they decide that these difficulties must have a spiritual basis. Consequently, they reason that they would not have these problems "if I were just a better disciple," "if I only prayed harder," "if I were more spiritual" or "if I only had better quiet times."

Just as baptism is not a cure for physical disease, becoming a disciple is not a vaccination against disorders of mental health. Unfortunately, the line that divides mental illness from spiritual illness is far narrower than the one that separates spiritual illness from physical disease. Therefore, the big question faced by all disciples with mental or emotional problems is "How much is sin, and how much is psychological?" Hopefully, reading this book will help disciples—the long-suffering Christians, as well as those who undertake to help them—be able to distinguish the difference.

Our Fallen World

It is an irrefutable fact that many mental and psychiatric disorders have a biological or "constitutional" basis. Modern science has shown us that behaviors and emotions are governed by a number of complicated neurological and biochemical processes. As we will discuss in later chapters, many mental illnesses are the result of one or more of these processes going awry. In short, certain mental disorders are just as much a "disease" as diabetes, multiple sclerosis or cancer.

As a result of man's disobedience, described in Genesis chapter three, sin, disease and misery all entered the world. Through this disobedience man forfeited his opportunity to live in a world without sickness. Thus, everyone who now inhabits this planet is subject to physical, social, emotional and spiritual hardships—a world of risk. The apostle Paul, however, taught us that the key to being an effective Christian is to learn to be "content in any and every situation, whether well fed or hungry, whether living in plenty or in want" (Philippians 4:12). He also wrote, "I can do everything through him who gives me strength" (Philippians 4:13). Therefore, even the disciple who suffers from one of these biologically based psychiatric disorders is not absolved from the responsibility of putting his or her challenge into spiritual context and learning to stay faithful to God.

John chapter nine tells the story of a man who was born blind. Quick to ascribe this to sin, Jesus' disciples asked who was at fault, the man (even though his blindness clearly predated his ability to sin) or his parents. Jesus then taught his disciples that the man was born with this congenital condition so that "the work of God might be displayed in his life" (John 9:3) through a miraculous healing. In 2 Corinthians 12:7-10, Paul, talking about his own condition (possibly a medical one), explained that he was refused the same kind of miraculous healing so that God's power could be made "perfect in weakness." In both cases, disease occurred independently of sin for the sole purpose of glorifying God and testifying to his power. If you struggle with psychiatric or emotional problems, you can still be a witness to God's greatness through the way you live your life!

We have established that because of man's fall from grace, diseases can occur independently of sin. However, this in no way lessens the disciple's responsibility to do his part to deal with sin in his life, disease or not. In John 5, Jesus healed an invalid who was reluctant to get well. Following this most miraculous healing, Jesus firmly admonished him to "stop sinning or something worse may happen to you" (John 5:14). It is a balance: The disciple has to assume both medical and spiritual responsibility for himself.

Hezekiah's Healing

God has provided us with some excellent examples of this in the Old Testament. Remember King Hezekiah? In 2 Kings 18:2 we read that he was king of Judah for twenty-nine years. During a period of time wherein most of the kings of Judah and Israel were stiff-necked and disobedient toward God, Hezekiah shined as one who:

> ...trusted in the Lord, the God of Israel. There was no one like him among all the kings of Judah, either before him or after him. He held fast to the Lord and did not cease to follow him; he kept the commands the Lord had given Moses. (2 Kings 18:5-6)

He became deathly ill at the tender young age of only thirty-seven or thirty-eight. We do not know the precise nature of his illness, although contextual evidence suggests that he was dying of some kind of localized infection or complications from a boil (2 Kings 20:7).

On his deathbed, this righteous and faithful man dared to pray to the Lord and ask for years to be added to his life. God, through the prophet Isaiah, responded by telling Hezekiah, "I have heard your prayer and seen your tears; I will heal you" (2 Kings 20:5). This is truly amazing! God rewarded Hezekiah's faithful prayer with a promise, a covenant, a virtual guarantee for a miraculous healing! Most of us would have rested fairly comfortably at that point, secure in the knowledge that the Lord Almighty, Creator of the Universe, had just filled out the ultimate spiritual prescription. However, Isaiah, acting as the "pharmacist" through whom God's prescriptions were filled, commanded those tending Hezekiah to prepare a poultice of figs and apply this remedy to the wound (2 Kings 20:7). As a result, Hezekiah recovered and continued to lead Judah for another fifteen years!

There is no question who affected Hezekiah's healing. It was the work of God, abetted by the king's faith, pure and simple. Still, a known medical remedy also had to be applied. Why did God work this way? This is something we will have to ask him ourselves one day. In the meantime, it is evident that the Lord works through doctors and medicines to heal people, as his wisdom dictates. What is the responsibility of a disciple who is ill? He or she needs to stay faithful, pray, seek medical attention and comply with medical treatment when it is recommended.

Of course, there is no guarantee that the doctors we consult have the ear of God, as Isaiah did. Therefore the one seeking treatment must always make an informed decision about what treatments are best. To this end, some of the material in later chapters of this book will enable disciples to make wise choices about medical and psychotherapeutic treatment.

Asa's Affliction

While the story of Hezekiah helps us to see that divine healing does not necessarily preclude medical treatment, the story of Asa illustrates how one can come to rely on medicine too much, sometimes to the exclusion of God. Asa was also a king of Judah, one who "did what was good and right in the eyes of the Lord his God" (2 Chronicles 14:2). He is renowned as the king who took the ultimate stand against the detestable pagan practices of his day, to the point of putting to death those who would not seek the Lord. Yet in his last years of life, he became too self-reliant, and his commitment began to lag. Faced with the threat of attack from the king of Israel, Asa used money to enlist the help of the king of Aram against his enemies. He did not seek God's counsel—in fact he imprisoned the prophet who confronted him with his lack of humility! Consequently, God afflicted him with a foot disease in the hopes that this would bring him to repentance. However, the Word tells us that "though his disease was severe, even in his illness he did not seek help from the Lord, but only from the physicians" (2 Chronicles 16:12). This resulted in his demise within two years.

Through Spiritual Eyes

Mental illness: Is it sin, or is it psychological? Through our years of practice it has occurred to us that all diseases—especially psychiatric ones like depression and anxiety—have both physical and spiritual components. The disciple's task is to attend to the former without neglecting the latter. God can use disease to call disciples to repentance, to challenge our faith or even to discipline us. At the same time, he can use illness to display his power and glory in our lives, provided that we remain sensitive to the spiritual issues involved. Daily exposure to the Word and the fellowship is what helps the disciple to recognize and deal with those spiritual issues (Hebrews 5:14).

To help the disciple recognize and identify psychiatric conditions that have a medical basis, we offer the following several chapters.

2

An Introduction to Psychiatric Disorders

Although they did not have fancy, technical names for them in Biblical times, many diseases are seen, mentioned and discussed in the Bible. Some sound like they may have involved mental or psychological disorders.

Biblical Illustrations

For example, one Scripture commentary postulates that the Gerasene demoniac was actually "...a man suffering from a manic-depressive psychosis associated with demon possession, which gave him an uncanny insight into who Jesus was."[1] Sure enough, the demoniac exhibited the depression, agitation and self-mutilative tendencies that sometimes characterize what we now refer to as "bipolar disorder."

Similarly, some commentators have philosophized that King Nebuchadnezzar, having been reduced to living like an animal and eating grass because of his pride (Daniel 4:33), was actually suffering from a disorder known as "lycanthropy" (the insane delusion that one has become a wolf!). Nebuchadnezzar himself said that his "sanity was restored" when he finally lifted his eyes to heaven (v 34).

[1]D. Guthrie and J.A. Motyer, Eds. *The New Bible Commentary Revised* (Grand Rapids: Wm. B. Eeardmans, Pub. Co., 1981), 902.

Did you ever wonder why Jeremiah is referred to as "the weeping prophet"? Sure, he was given the odious task of pronouncing judgment against his own people and foretelling their doom, which was certainly not the most cheerful of tasks. However, he was also prone to self-analysis and self-criticism (see Jeremiah 10:24, for example), possibly indicative of a mild form of depression that we refer to as "dysthymia."

How about King Saul? After he fell out of God's favor, Saul suffered from intense melancholic episodes which were accompanied by what appear to be (at least from the perspective of a psychologist) some kind of migraine headache variant! Only the soothing sounds of David's harp would relieve Saul's suffering and dispel the evil spirit (1 Samuel 16:15-23). Those of you who suffer from migraines will have no trouble making a conceptual connection between your headaches and evil demons! Today it is known that migraines and depression often coexist, and the same medication is sometimes used to treat both.

The two of us have often joked about the number of people in the Bible who seem to have shown a conspicuous, but apparently God-inspired, lack of impulse control. One who comes to mind is Samson, who caught three hundred foxes, tied their tails together and used them to set fire to the fields of the Philistines (Judges 15:4-6). Had Samson been around in our time, it is almost certain that someone would have referred him to our office for evaluation of a conduct disorder or an attention deficit/hyperactivity disorder. Ritalin may have been used as an alternative treatment to hair removal as a way of getting him to settle down!

Establishing Standards

Since well before the days of Sigmund Freud, the medical world has been struggling to identify and classify all psychiatric disorders and establish standards to make them easier to identify and diagnose. At first most psychiatric disorders were given demeaning, "politically incorrect" names like "idiocy" and "insanity." These terms reflected science's lack of understanding of the nature and causes of these disorders. They promoted a sense of fear and distaste toward the mentally ill that has persisted to this day and has done little to encourage people to seek help for possible mental problems. Behavioral scientists have since endeavored to make mental illnesses more understandable and less threatening through research and education. The fruit of that labor currently takes the form of the *Diagnostic and Statistical Manual of Mental Disorders,* now in its fourth edition, published by the American Psychiatric Association (APA).[2] The DSM-IV, as it's called, is a compendium of every known psychiatric disorder on the planet. It's a favorite joke around our office that almost any person in the world, if they were to browse through the DSM-IV long enough, would find some diagnosis that would describe them! The illnesses covered by the DSM-IV range from the obscure (for example "trichotillomania," or compulsive hair pulling) to the well known (like depression, schizophrenia and panic disorder).

For each disorder the DSM-IV outlines a list of identifying signs and symptoms, plus some useful information regarding prevalence estimates (how many people are thought to suffer from the disorder) and expected complications. The DSM-IV is not exhaustive, nor is it one hundred percent useful and accurate. However, it represents the best efforts of psychiatric research and science to systematically classify mental disorders.

Axis I and II Disorders

The DSM-IV makes a distinction between two general types of mental diseases. The first type, called Axis I disorders, entails mental disorders that are understood to be caused at least

[2]American Psychiatric Association (APA), *Diagnostic and Statistical Manual of Mental Disorders,* 4th ed. (Washington, D.C.: APA, 1994).

in part by biological or neurological factors. For the most part, you are not born with Axis I disorders. Instead, they usually begin at some particular point in childhood, adolescence or adulthood. Because they are at least partly biological in nature, medication is usually used as a component of treatment. Axis I disorders include major depression, post-traumatic stress disorder, generalized anxiety disorder, attention deficit/hyperactivity disorder and chronic pain disorder. They also include most of the strictly childhood disorders, such as learning disorders, oppositional-defiant disorder, autism and enuresis (bedwetting). Alcohol dependence and substance abuse, which are considered mental diseases in the DSM-IV, are also included on Axis I.

The other group of disorders, so-called Axis II disorders, involves mental retardation diagnoses, plus some disorders that are considered "characterological" in nature. These "personality disorders" are much harder to treat, because they are related to maladaptive aspects of the personality. In other words, they are syndromes of dysfunctional personality traits that make it extremely difficult for the individual to get along with others and get by in the world.

Generally speaking, Axis II disorders cannot be treated with a pill or potion. In our experience, the only way an individual can be "cured" of a personality disorder is to gain insight into the problem and then make a decision to change. At that point the therapist or mental health professional can assist the person by "arming" that person with special techniques or methods to improve the way he or she deals with the world. How rarely this happens! How rare it is in the world that such persons willingly acknowledge and deal with deeply ingrained, dysfunctional aspects of their characters. It is for this reason that the majority of our colleagues refuse to even try to treat Axis II disorders. However, praise God that this is precisely what disciples are trained to do!

True Christians are willing to humble out, become vulnerable and fight hard to change whatever is ungodly or hindering them in their characters (see Ephesians 4:22-24 and Hebrews 12:1). Unlike patients in the world, they also have the help of the Holy Spirit (Romans 8:9, 26-27). This is why we, as psychologists, can safely say that we have actually seen disciples overcome and conquer these so-called personality disorders that are considered intractable in the world of psychiatry.

'Disorder' Defined

So what is a "disorder," anyway? Generally speaking, mental health professionals consider a disorder to be a pattern of symptoms that causes "marked distress" and/or interferes significantly with some aspect of daily life (usually social, school or occupational functioning). In addition, the DSM-IV states that this pattern of symptoms "...must not be merely an expectable and culturally sanctioned response to a particular event, for example, the death of a loved one" (APA 1994, xxi). In other words, the symptoms are not the product of the normal vicissitudes of life.

This definition of "mental disorder" makes sense to most people. Usually, people who have a mental illness experience symptoms that they find personally upsetting or distressing, such as the episodes of despair that characterize major depression or the irresistible, irrational impulses that characterize obsessive-compulsive disorder. However, it should be kept in mind that almost all mental disorders fall along a continuum of severity, from mild to moderate to incapacitating. As noted in the first chapter, it is our experience that most disciples do not like to admit that they are stressed or incapacitated beyond what they can bear, because they consider it indulgent or a sign of spiritual weakness. They prefer the white-knuckle approach, which involves trying to tough it out until they become sufficiently "spiritual." This sometimes results in years of unnecessary misery.

A good rule of thumb for seeking treatment is as follows: If you think you have a problem, then it *might* be a problem. If you do not think you have a problem, but those who love you think you do, then it still *might* be a problem. The only way to know for sure is to seek out a qualified mental health professional and have it checked out. In Chapter 7, we'll offer some advice about what type of clinician should be chosen out of the vast array of available mental health professionals.

Multiple Factors

At this point, some attention needs to be paid to the interplay between heredity, biology and environmental factors. Most of the Axis I disorders that we will discuss have some basis in biology. Many are caused by deficiencies in certain neurotransmitters, which are the chemicals that permit communication between the approximately one hundred billion cells in the human brain. The predisposition toward this neurochemical deficiency is often inherited. In other words, a person is more likely to have one of these disorders if he or she has a parent or other family member with the disorder. Is this a guarantee? Not necessarily. Most often, the chemical imbalance is triggered by some stressful event, which could be anything from the death of a family pet to an incident of physical abuse. Interestingly, the research tells us that the earlier this imbalance is treated or corrected (usually with an appropriate psychoactive medication, such as an antidepressant or antianxiety agent), the less likely another episode of the disorder is later on. This is why we advocate early identification and treatment of mental or emotional problems—as early as childhood.

Because these disorders have a biological component, many people who suffer from a psychiatric problem would probably have developed it regardless of how they were raised. They would still be depressed (or anxious or psychotic) even if they were raised in a "perfect" home. At the same time, environmental stressors such as abuse, neglect, abandonment, divorce or other traumatic experiences may precipitate or trigger the first episode of a mental disorder.

Modern-Day Illustrations

We recall the case of one disciple, a forty-year-old man who had been in the ministry for some time. He came to the office stating that he had felt "joyless" for most of his life. Despite being a committed Christian who had solid faith in the Biblical promise of the "peace of God, which transcends all understanding" (Philippians 4:7), he reported that he had been unhappy for years. He had never been severely depressed, but he had never been severely happy, either. Eventually, he just decided that he was "incapable" of feeling happiness, and he labored under this assumption ("going through the motions") for some time. Fortunately, he came to the realization that this could not possibly be part of God's plan for one of the saints, and he sought help.

Part of what prevented this brother from doing anything sooner was his consternation about the reasons for his unhappiness. He had an terrific wife, two beautiful children (one of whom was studying the Bible), a nice home and a good job. He was not living in poverty, and to his knowledge he had never been abused or mistreated. He felt—rightly so—that he had no good reason to be depressed, so he assumed that his lack of joy was just some kind of ingratitude on his part.

A clinical history revealed that there were other members of this disciple's extended family who had suffered from depression in the past. In fact his paternal grandfather, whom he had never known, had been hospitalized for psychiatric reasons and eventually committed suicide. There was also a paternal uncle who had been an alcoholic in the 1930s (back then, when little was known about depression, many people became alcoholics by trying to "self-medicate" their depression). It was clear that this well-meaning and dedicated brother had a strong hereditary predisposition toward depression. A full load, if you will, of mood disorders were floating around in his gene pool! As we would have with any medical disorder with a genetic component—diabetes or heart disease, for example—we made recommendations for appropriate treatment (antidepressant medication, in this case), and the brother has been fine ever since. He often states that his biggest regret is that he did not look into this problem sooner.

This was a fairly clear-cut case of a mostly biologically based problem. More often, however, psychiatric problems represent a combination of biological and environmental factors. For example, we are reminded of the case of a twenty-three-year-old Christian who was referred to the office by a friend because of unpredictable fits of rage that were completely out of proportion to the events that elicited them. As it turns out, this disciple had a brother who had been treated in the past for manic-depressive illness (a.k.a. bipolar disorder). Over the years, this sibling had put the family through all kinds of turmoil, including setting the family's home on fire. Clearly, our patient had a significant history of trauma and stress in addition to his own genetic predilection to depression and psychotic symptoms. These had to be dealt with extensively through a combination of medication, therapy and loving, patient discipling.

We hope that these stories illustrate how naïve it is to view an emotional problem as strictly spiritual or strictly biological. Even the most committed Christian must confront the possibility that he or she may be suffering from a biologically based illness that is out of his or her control. Conversely, it is to the detriment of the medical community that the spiritual component of mental illness is so often ignored. This is why, in our opinion, no one with a psychiatric problem will ever be completely "cured" unless he also turns his life over to Christ and agrees to live by God's word. We often say that without God, the most we can offer our patients—through medication and therapy—is to help them learn how to survive and "tolerate" life. In contrast, Christians can hold to the promise that they *will* overcome and one day "eat from the tree of life, which is in the paradise of God" (Revelation 2:7). In the meantime, we urge you to become educated Christians who are committed to God but also know something about the psychiatric illnesses that entered the world as a result of man's sin.

3

Mood Disorders

What are some of these biologically based disorders that confuse and confound the picture when there are disciples with emotional or psychiatric problems? Presented in the next few chapters is our own small compendium of some of the most common psychiatric diseases, pared down and simplified for your perusal. This synopsis is far from exhaustive, but will hopefully help you to recognize some of the disorders we are discussing based on what they look like, what causes them and how they are treated.

The term "mood disorders" includes disturbances of mood that are in excess of, or cannot be explained by, the usual changes in mood that accompany the normal tribulations of life. We are not talking about "the blues"—grief reactions following the loss of a loved one, or the normally expected reactions to stressful events (sometimes called "reactive sadness"). Instead, this is a clinical syndrome caused by deficient production of at least two known neurotransmitters, serotonin and norepinephrine. Imbalances in the processes governed by these two chemicals cause the following symptoms:

- A continuous, pervasive feeling of emptiness or sadness that cannot be explained, or that does not seem to be in

proportion to whatever stresses are being experienced at
the time

- Impaired functioning at school or on the job; strained
  relationships with others
- Impaired attention and concentration
- Erosion of self-esteem
- Changes in sleep, appetite, activity level and/or sex drive:
  Usually, depressed individuals complain of fatigue, lack
  of energy, reduced capacity for feeling pleasure and a
  decline in the ability to enjoy previously enjoyed activities (such as hobbies or other interests). They sleep or
  eat excessively (or, sometimes, not enough). Unexplain-
  able physical complaints may arise, such as headaches
  or stomachaches. Taken together, these are referred to
  as "vegetative symptoms."

Major Depression

What most people do not know is that depression takes
different forms. Although all forms of depression share these
symptoms, depression works over a number of different
timelines, at different levels of severity. For example, major
depressive disorder, which is the most familiar form of the
disease, is an episodic phenomenon that is characterized by
distinct periods of severe, incapacitating depression and sadness. These episodes, which may or may not be triggered by
anything in particular, often entail suicidal thoughts or behaviors. For this reason, people in the midst of a major depressive
episode sometimes have to be hospitalized in order to ensure
their safety. These episodes can last days, weeks or months.
However, by definition, one must experience most of the symptoms outlined above for at least two weeks in order to qualify
for the diagnosis of major depressive episode.

Some people experience major depression only once in their
lifetime. This is referred to as "major depressive disorder, single

episode." Other people experience recurrent episodes, separated by periods of "normal" functioning that can also last for months or years. Such individuals are said to be suffering from "depressive disorder, recurrent." Regardless of how many episodes the person experiences in his or her life, each one is assigned a description of its severity, either mild, moderate or severe.

As suggested earlier, a distinction must be made between major depression and reactive sadness, which is the normally expected emotional reaction to a stressful or depressing event. All of us experience this kind of depression at one time or another, but it rarely lasts for more than a few days and usually does not interfere significantly with normal day-to-day functioning.

Also, major depression is different from grief, which is a normal response to loss. Incidentally, the loss need not always involve the death of a loved one. Divorce or other forms of permanent separation can cause the same reaction. The symptoms of grief mimic many of those in major depression, but there is usually not the corresponding loss of self-esteem. Although antidepressant medication is sometimes used for a short time when someone is grieving, time and an abiding trust in God are the preferred remedies. With the help of these remedies, Job was able to move from cursing the day of his birth (Job 3:1) to joy and prosperity following the loss of his children and virtually all of his material possessions.

Dysthymia

There is another form of depression that receives far less press than major depression because it is much harder to recognize. However, this form of depression, known as "dysthymic disorder," is just as destructive and demoralizing, if not more so. Dysthymic disorder, a.k.a. "dysthymia," is more of a low-level, chronic, less severe but more persistent version of depression. By definition, persons with dysthymia suffer from depressed mood for the majority of days over a period of at least two years. While depressed, the patient with dysthymia may experience fatigue, loss of energy (known as "anergia"), diminished self-esteem, disrupted appetite, impaired concentration and/or feelings of hopelessness. However, these symptoms are not of such severity as to interfere substantially with family, social, educational or occupational functioning. It was this condition that led the forty-year-old disciple, described in the previous chapter, to resign himself to being "unhappy" for most of his life.

We have often surmised that dysthymia is one of Satan's preferred tools for gradually wearing down the resistance of the disciple's soul. Since it does not involve the catastrophic, incapacitating experiences that characterize major depression, it is stealthy and insidious. Disciples recognize their perpetual feelings of hopelessness and joylessness, even when things are going well, but since they are still able to function, they decide that these feelings are surely the sign of a weak faith. Therefore they seek no treatment, and the gradual erosion of faith and self-esteem continues. This is particularly sad for us as psychologists, because dysthymia is relatively easy to treat. It is depressing for *us* to think about the number of "walking wounded" in God's kingdom who could be helped.

Bipolar Disorder
The last mood disorder that bears discussion in this book is the one now known as bipolar disorder. In its former life this disorder was also known as manic-depression or manic-depressive psychosis. Traditionally, bipolar disorder refers to episodes of depression alternating with episodes of "mania"—a period of extreme elation, euphoria or agitation. People experiencing a manic episode usually have racing thoughts and feel tireless or extremely energetic. In fact some manic episodes last for days, during which the person does not sleep at all and

accomplishes a great deal (provided he or she can stay organized enough to complete anything). The person talks excessively (pressured speech) and is almost impossible to interrupt. Unlike depression, a person in the midst of a manic episode experiences "grandiosity" or inflated self-esteem. He or she will engage in unrestrained behaviors that reflect this, such as gambling, promiscuous sexual behavior, impulsive buying sprees or the capricious giving away of money. Patients have said they feel almost superhuman during these episodes. Because this is such a pleasant change from depression, they often value their mania and consequently, resist treatment. Unfortunately, the manic episode often (but not always) ends in an equally intense episode of profound depression and despair. Bipolar patients refer to this as "the crash." The movie *Mr. Jones*, starring Richard Gere, presents an excellent portrayal of the bipolar process.

Typically, episodes of mania and depression last anywhere from several days to several months in the person with bipolar disorder. These episodes are often interspersed with periods of normal mood. If there are two or more episodes of both depression and mania within a calendar year, the condition is referred to as "rapid cycling" bipolar disorder. There are other variants of this disorder, such as bipolar II disorder (depression alternating with episodes of less intense mania, or "hypomania") and mixed bipolar disorder (in which symptoms of mania and depression are experienced simultaneously). In any event, bipolar disorder can be a devastating illness that often results in financial, occupational or social disaster.

Diagnosing Mood Disorders

Even with these detailed (but admittedly unscientific) descriptions, it may be unclear as to whether or not you are suffering from a mood disorder. Unfortunately, there are no reliable biological tests for major depression, dysthymia or bipolar disorder. There is no simple blood test or laboratory procedure that can accurately identify any of these illnesses. Instead, diagnosing a mood disorder is a process that should include a thorough clinical interview (by a qualified mental health professional) and psychological testing, as necessary. Since these disorders are at least to some degree hereditary, part of the clinical interview should focus on whether or not other family members have ever suffered from a mood disorder. This is sometimes a difficult question to answer because most of our extended family members (grandparents, aunts, uncles, etc.) lived in a time when little was known about psychiatric problems, and families were hesitant to admit that anyone suffered from a mental disorder. As noted earlier, before the days of antidepressant medications, people suffering from depression often tried to medicate themselves with alcohol. This is why a history of alcoholism on the part of any grandparent, great-uncle or other distant family member may signify a hereditary predisposition to depression.

Another important part of the diagnostic interview process is the patient's medical history. Before a firm diagnosis of a mood disorder can be made, medical disorders that mimic or cause depressive or manic symptoms must first be ruled out. These include the following:

- AIDS
- Brain tumors
- Encephalitis
- Diabetes
- Hyperthyroidism or hypothyroidism
- Hepatitis
- PMS
- Multiple sclerosis
- Epstein-Barre virus (chronic fatigue syndrome)
- Lupus (systemic lupus erythematosis)

• Drug abuse (especially amphetamines, cocaine and steroids, which cause manic symptoms; and narcotics, alcohol and barbiturates, which feign depression)

These are conditions that *can* be detected through various lab tests. Therefore, a complete physical, with attendant bloodwork, should be done first whenever a mood disorder is suspected. Also, an analysis of all other medications being taken by the patient must be made, since certain drugs can actually cause depressive symptoms. These include corticosteroids, antihypertensives (blood pressure medication), hormone supplements and birth control pills. As we will discuss in Chapter 7, the process of diagnosis and treatment is a team approach that should involve the patient, the primary care physician and the mental health specialist.

Treatments with Medications

So, what treatments are available for those suffering from mood disorders, once an appropriate diagnosis has been made? For disciples especially, we tend to use a three-step approach to treatment: By reading this book you are taking one of these steps, which is to try to put your illness into a spiritual context. The Bible studies in Chapter 11 should prove helpful in this regard. Chapter 7 should be useful in understanding the next step, which involves finding a therapist to help you change the thinking and behaviors that contribute to your mood disorder. The third step involves medication, which is usually necessary as a way of managing the biochemical components of depression, dysthymia and bipolar disorder. The role of counseling and psychotherapy will be dealt with later.

Knowledge regarding the causes and best treatments of mood disorders has grown tremendously over the last fifteen or twenty years. Prior to that time, when depression was viewed as a "neurosis" that stemmed from an individual's ability to cope with stress or trauma, addictive sedatives or tranquilizers (such as Valium) were often prescribed, thereby contributing to widespread abuse of these medications. Electroconvulsive therapy (ECT or "shock therapy")—which is still useful in cases of severe, intractable depression—was used extensively after World War II. Eventually, medications specific to the biochemistry of depression were devised. Many of these are still in use today.

However, 1988 marked the beginning of a new era in antidepressant medication when Prozac hit the shelves! It was the first of a class of medications which treat depression by targeting serotonin, one of those neurotransmitters that are known to be deficient in cases of depression. Prozac and similar medications that have arisen since then work by making more serotonin available for brain cells to use. These medications are collectively referred to as Selective Serotonin Reuptake Inhibitors (SSRIs). Because they deal with only certain specific neurochemicals and brain cells, they are potent antidepressants that cause far fewer side effects than traditional antidepressants in persons who are suffering from "true" biochemically based depression. Consequently, they became very popular very fast. In turn this led to a good deal of misuse and overprescription, sometimes to people with conditions other than depression who had no business being treated with an antidepressant. Untoward reactions to Prozac followed, as did the lawsuits that were so prevalent for a time following Prozac's heyday.

Since then, a number of similar medications have appeared which have loosened Prozac's monopoly on the antidepressant market. Some of these medications target other neurotransmitters, such as norepinephrine, thereby making them even more effective for some people. Many of these medications are also beneficial in the treatment of other psychiatric disorders, such as anxiety or obsessive-compulsive disorder. Here is a partial list of medications that are commonly used in the treatment of mood disorders:

Brand Name	Generic Name
Prozac	fluoxetine
Zoloft	sertraline
Paxil	paroxetine
Effexor	venlafaxine
Tofranil	imipramin
Norpramin	desipramine
Desyrel	trazodone
Elavil	amitriptyline
Wellbutrin	bupropion
Serzone	nefazodone

The patient needs to keep in mind that "psychopharmacology," the use of medications to treat mental illnesses, is not an exact science—each person's biological system is unique because of differences in size, weight, metabolism, liver function and other variables. Also, antidepressants each have different properties which may be more suitable to some patients than others. For example, Desyrel is a sedating antidepressant, while Prozac has a stimulating or "activating" effect. Therefore, we always caution patients that treating depression is sometimes an experimental process. Various medications, dosages and dosing schedules sometimes need to be tried before an effective medical treatment is found for the individual patient, depending on that patient's physiology and particular constellation of symptoms. This sometimes calls for much forbearance (maybe this is why they are called "patients"). Be willing to work with your doctor or therapist until a "best fit" medication is found.

It should be noted that treatment with an antidepressant is never intended as a long-term therapy. Unlike using insulin to treat diabetes, it is not a "given" that a patient must take an antidepressant for the rest of his or her life. Usually, the plan is to take the medication for at least nine to twelve months. At the end of that period, medication may be tapered off slowly if all members of the "treatment team"—patient, physician and/ or therapist—see fit. Some patients never need to take the medication again. Some patients may go for years until a stressful event, such as a financial problem or the loss of a loved one, precipitates another depressive episode that requires medical treatment. However, there are those rare patients that plummet into a depression any time an attempt is made to withdraw the medication. These patients may need to remain on an antidepressant for life.

As far as medical science can tell, the earlier a depressive illness is dealt with medically, the less likely it is that the patient will experience a recurrence of depression later in life. The analogy we like to use is that of digging a ditch: Each time an episode of depression occurs, the biochemical "ditch" gets deeper and more difficult to fill. Once again, this is why we encourage anyone who even thinks that they might be suffering from a mood disorder to seek help. The earlier that treatment for depression is sought, the lower the probability that treatment will be a lifetime proposition.

Natural Treatments

Before we close out this discussion on mood disorders, mention should be made of God's "natural antidepressants." Some are sold over the counter in a bottle, such as the increasingly popular St. John's Wort (the herb, hypericum perforatum) and so-called SAM-e, which is a naturally occurring substance in everyone's body but which was first produced as a pharmaceutical by an Italian firm in the 1970s. Since then more than forty clinical studies have been done, mostly in Europe, showing the efficacy of SAM-e in treating depressive syndromes.[1] Both St. John's Wort and SAM-e are, in fact, effective for some people in the treatment of mild depression. In particular, St. John's Wort seems to work best as a preventative if taken regularly by people who are prone to mild depression. However, we always caution patients that just because something is natural does not mean it lacks the potential for harm! Even herbal remedies present some risk of unfavorable side effects or interaction with other medications you might be taking. At the risk of sounding like a television ad, always check with your family doctor before you start a course of herbal treatment.

There are other natural antidepressants that are even less risky and certainly far more fun than herbal remedies. One of these is exercise. Physical exertion has been shown to stimulate the production of endorphins and enkephalins, which are the brain's natural painkillers and mood enhancers. It also helps eliminate physical factors that contribute to depression, such as obesity and hypertension. For these reasons, regular exercise has always been used as a first-line treatment for depression.

Another natural antidepressant is the pursuit of a hobby or field of interest, for no other reason but to have fun and forget about your troubles. It has occurred to us that many disciples suffer from a kind of kingdom-martyrdom complex, wherein they dedicate themselves wholeheartedly to the service of God and family. To such dedicated Christians the pursuit of a hobby seems like a frivolous waste of that increasingly scarce commodity, time. Consequently, they relinquish the sport or hobby or artistic talent that used to bring them such joy and pleasure. How can this lead to anything but resentment at some level?

It is a fundamental teaching of Ecclesiastes that we are to enjoy what life has to offer, as long as we keep these

[1]For more information about SAM-e, see *Stop Depression Now: SAM-e, The Breakthrough Substance* by Dr. Richard Brown (New York: G. P. Putnam and Sons, 1999).

pleasures in perspective and never let them supplant our love of God (see, for example, Ecclesiastes 11:8-10). What a shame it is to deny ourselves "permission" to do something fun! Keep in mind that as a result of doing something fun and healthy, you will be more pleasant to be around anyway, thereby making you a more effective Christian. If you still need an even more compelling reason to have fun, bear in mind that your sports or hobbies can become evangelistic opportunities in themselves. In case you have not noticed, gyms, golf courses, dance studios, museums, quilting bees, basketball courts, bridge tables, hiking trails, baseball diamonds and antique shops are all full of people!

No two people have developed deeper convictions about this point than the authors of this book. Mary was (and still is) a talented ballerina who danced with her school's ballet troupe all through college and later taught ballet at night to earn extra money during graduate school. However, over the subsequent years this first love gradually took a distant backseat to children, husband, church and career. She eventually decided that her life would never have room for ballet again. Several years later she developed the conviction that getting back into ballet might be just what the doctor (in this case, her husband) ordered in order to combat her feelings of overwhelming stress. She now goes joyfully and guiltlessly to an adult ballet class three to four times a week.

Similarly, Michael leaves his office promptly at noon three days a week and dedicates his lunch hour to his hobby, Tae Kwon Do. This time has been set in stone and is guarded as jealously and possessively as Sunday morning church. We both love having a certain time in the day where the *only* things we have to think about are how to get more extension on that front kick or arabesque. In addition to our individual pursuits of ballet and Tae Kwon Do, we also take a ballroom dance class together at least one night a week. Although this might be inconvenient at times from a scheduling standpoint, the antidepressant effects (as well as the benefits to the marriage) make it well worth the time!

Keep in mind that your particular interest need not involve a sport or other physical activity. Painting, photography, chess, music, model making, arts and crafts—just about anything that is enjoyed as a hobby can have an antidepressant effect, as long as you make the same commitment to it as you would to taking medication. In other words, having fun is a necessity, not an option! It is one part of a comprehensive plan to battle and prevent depression.

Having once been a controversial disorder about which little is known, depression has more recently become the scourge of the twentieth century. The prevalence of depression in this century—and in particular the last twenty years—has been amplified by our stressed-out, unspiritual society. However, as our knowledge about mood disorders increases by leaps and bounds, so does our arsenal of treatments. Christians need not suffer from depression as long as they are willing to trust God, trust the medical advances that God has permitted, and work patiently at getting well.

4

Anxiety Disorders

Like mood disorders, anxiety disorders are of many types which vary in severity and in the degree to which they interfere with daily life. However, all anxiety disorders are thought to have something to do with a malfunction of the neurological and physiological systems that govern the body's "normal" response to stress. Therefore, before we can talk about anxiety disorders, we must first turn our attention to the topic of stress and the effect that it exerts on the body.

Fight or Flight

God has endowed us with a very basic, primitive "emergency response system" that helps us deal with dangerous situations. When human beings (and most mammals) perceive a threatening situation, a number of things occur quickly and automatically at a physical level. The brain, having interpreted the threat of danger, sends a message to the adrenal glands, which are located on top of the kidneys. In response, these glands secrete adrenaline, which is a super-energizing neurochemical that causes a number of almost immediate changes in the body. Pupils dilate, the heart begins working more quickly, breathing rate increases, digestive activity slows down, sweat glands start cranking—all to prepare the body to either fight the threat or (if you'll pardon the indelicate expression) run like the devil! Psychologists and physiologists refer to this as the "fight or flight" response.

After the crisis has been settled one way or another, the body returns to its normal state. However, every stressful event also causes the production of "stress hormones" such as cortisol that, over time, have a harmful effect on the body. For instance, these stress hormones have been found to wear away at the muscle tissue of the heart, which partly accounts for the relationship between stress and heart attacks.

Stress 101

Fortunately, we live in a time in which most of us are no longer confronted with major threats to our physical safety on a daily basis. For example, it is fairly uncommon, at least in the United States, to be confronted with a lion or a bear while on our way to work. However, we do encounter modern stressful situations that actually induce the same physiological response. One of the authors of this book (who will remain nameless) struggles almost daily with this stress response in reaction to slow traffic and inept drivers. Similarly, most of us will experience the same physiological stress symptoms (sweating, palpitations, muscular tension and an increase in blood pressure) when we are called in to the boss's office, when our children are fighting or when we suddenly remember that we have a test at school today for which we are not prepared. Other people experience this stress reaction regularly in response to much more serious situations, such as living with a physically abusive spouse or family member. Some of our brothers and sisters, especially in other countries, must endure actual threats to their lives and well being on a daily basis.

Back in the days when typical stress involved meeting up with a lion or bear on the way to the sheep pasture, the act of dealing with the situation—either by fighting it or running from it—helped to dissipate the adrenaline and cortisol in the body, thereby avoiding the harmful long-term effects of these substances. Unfortunately, modern man (and woman) has artfully learned to stuff the feelings of rage, aggression and reactive anger that are precipitated by the stress response. How many of us, when confronted by a boss for a job poorly done or a deadline that was left unmet, give in to the physiological urge to either run away or punch him in the nose? Instead, we have become sufficiently "civilized" to repress these urges. In turn we are left with a broiling mixture of adrenaline and cortisol coursing through our bodies, doing subtle but gradual damage to our heart muscle and wearing us down.

Of course, daily stress of this type is a disease that is common to man. In Ecclesiastes, Solomon makes the observation that "All his days his work is pain and grief; even at night his mind does not rest" (Ecclesiastes 2:23). At the same time, he admonishes us to try to resist the "fight or flight" response, especially in the workplace. For example, Ecclesiastes 10:4 reads, "If a ruler's anger rises against you, do not leave your post; calmness can lay great errors to rest." How can these two be reconciled? The answer to the question of how to deal with normal daily stress is beyond the scope of this book—entire volumes could be written on the stress-reducing properties of daily prayer, regular exercise (which reduces the levels of stress hormones in the blood) and the companionship of friends who allow you to vent your frustrations onto them. Instead, we will confine our discussion to stress and anxiety symptoms that exceed the norm.

Symptoms of Anxiety Disorders

As suggested earlier, anxiety (which can be defined as the state of uneasiness that accompanies stress) becomes a disorder when there is a malfunction in the normal stress-response system. Most anxiety disorders share the following symptoms:

- Restlessness and muscular tension
- Shortness of breath or the feeling of suffocation
- Racing heartbeat
- Sweating
- Lightheadedness
- Difficulty falling asleep
- Feeling of impending dread or doom
- Problems with attention and concentration[1]

Panic Disorder

Sometimes these symptoms occur in the form of very intense episodes that last for anywhere from a few seconds to thirty minutes. These episodes, which often occur unexpectedly for no apparent reason, are referred to as "panic attacks." When these episodes occur repeatedly, in such a way as to interfere significantly with normal social, educational or occupational functioning, the individual is said to be suffering from a panic disorder.

According to the DSM-IV, panic disorder occurs in somewhere between one to two percent of the population. Of these individuals, about one third to one half also experience "agoraphobia" during a panic attack. The DSM-IV defines agoraphobia as:

> "...anxiety about being in places or situations from which escape might be difficult (or embarrassing) or in which help may not be available in the event of having a panic attack or panic-like symptoms (e.g., fear of having a sudden attack of dizziness or a sudden attack of diarrhea)." (APA 1994, 396)

The anxiety typically leads to pervasive avoidance of a variety of situations that may include being alone outside of the home or being home alone; being in a crowd of people;

[1]Adapted from J. Preston and J. Johnson *Clinical Psychopharmacology Made Ridiculously Simple.* (Miami: MedMaster, 1994).

traveling in an automobile, bus or airplane; or being on a bridge or in an elevator. In other words, the individual avoids all situations in which he or she might have a panic attack.

As you can imagine, this can become quite incapacitating for some people, especially those who have made the commitment to "go and make disciples of all nations" (Matthew 28:19). How can someone reach out to others (seek and save the lost) when the very act of leaving the house or spending time in a car is terrifying? We will attempt to answer this question later in this chapter during our discussion on various treatments for anxiety disorders.

Generalized Anxiety Disorder

Panic disorder needs to be distinguished from another anxiety syndrome, namely generalized anxiety disorder. This involves chronic, longstanding, mild or lingering feelings of worry, apprehension or anxiety that are out of proportion to the stressors in the person's life. Such persons are usually described as chronic worriers who are overly concerned about almost every aspect of everyday life, such as finances, job responsibilities and family matters. In addition, they may spend much of their time dwelling on worrisome situations that have not even happened yet, but might happen at some point in the future. These worries may range from the possible but unlikely (for example, some deathly illness befalling themselves or a family member) to the illogical and completely irrational (such as being hit by a meteorite). Although the person is aware that these worries are excessive and irrational, he or she feels powerless to prevent the intrusion of these thoughts. As a result, the individual experiences fatigue, impaired concentration and other physiological symptoms of anxiety.

It is our impression that generalized anxiety is the disorder which is most likely to be misdiagnosed by other disciples as a lack of faith. All disciples—in fact, all human beings—worry. Worry is just an emotional response to our uncertainty about the future and our frustration over being unable to control all the circumstances of our daily lives. Worry triggers the physiological stress response known as anxiety. From a spiritual standpoint, "normal" feelings of worry and anxiety can be viewed as an incentive to rely on God, just as the perception of physical pain serves as an incentive to take the hand off a hot stove. This is why Jesus spent so much time teaching on the subject. In Matthew 6:25 he tells us:

> "Do not worry about your life, what you will eat or drink; or about your body, what you will wear. Is not life more important than food, and the body more important than clothes?"

Later in the same chapter he touches on the futility of worry by asking, "Who of you by worrying can add a single hour to his life?" (v27). He even portrays the act of worry as a pagan practice! (v32).

Since all disciples struggle with reconciling worry and faith, we are quick to attribute excessive worry in others to an unwillingness or inability to rely on God. This is most often the case. However, to quote the DSM-IV, the tendency to worry becomes a disorder when: "The anxiety, worry or physical symptoms cause clinically significant distress or impairment in social, occupational or other important areas of functioning" (APA 1994, 433). For example, we can think of one disciple who worried excessively about the safety of his children. He was constantly concerned that some disaster might befall them, or that they might fall victim to a sudden, life-threatening illness. This concern, although understandable in moderation, became incapacitating when he had to interrupt his work every five or ten minutes to call home and check on the children.

Phobias

Before we go on to our discussion of how to treat these problems, there are a few more anxiety syndromes that deserve some attention. Certain of these involve feelings of panic or anxiety only in reaction to very specific situations or objects and are therefore referred to as specific phobias. These phobias usually involve a reaction to a specific kind of animal (such as insects), some kind of natural or environmental phenomenon (such as storms, heights or water) or a certain situation (such as driving, flying or being in a tunnel). There is also the so-called social phobia, in which an individual experiences anxiety only when in social or interpersonal situations (for example, when speaking publicly or asking someone out on a date).

It would seem logical to assume that these phobias are born when someone has actually had an extremely embarrassing, traumatic or life-threatening encounter with a certain object or situation. This single experience would then predispose the individual to have the same fearful reaction every time he or she is placed in that situation in the future. However, specific phobias sometimes "just happen" for no apparent reason. For example, our youngest child has a mortal fear of tornadoes, even though she has never experienced one in her life. (Of course, having the movie *Twister* in our video collection might have something to do with this.)

Most specific phobias are relatively easy to treat. In therapy, we usually use a technique known as "systematic desensitization," wherein the patient is gradually taught to learn how to relax in the presence of the feared object.

Post-Traumatic Stress Disorder

At the same time, there is another kind of specific phobia that is more serious and damaging. This is known as post-traumatic stress disorder (PTSD). The DSM-IV describes this disorder as a constellation of anxiety symptoms following exposure to a traumatic event that evoked extreme feelings of fear, helplessness or horror. Such events might include violent personal assault (sexual or physical), robbery, kidnapping, incarceration or even being diagnosed with a life-threatening illness. Interestingly, these traumatic events need not have been experienced directly by the individual. Instead, the individual might develop PTSD symptoms after witnessing an event that resulted in someone else's death, harm or injury. This would account for the relatively high number of people who develop PTSD after serving their country during war.

In order to qualify for a diagnosis of PTSD, the person must continue to "re-experience" the traumatic event through recurrent dreams or vivid recollections that evoke the same feelings of fear or horror. These recollections can sometimes be triggered by exposure to events or circumstances that resemble the original trauma. Take, for example, the war veteran who ducks for cover and panics every time he hears a car backfire or a balloon pop. In addition, individuals with PTSD often avoid others or experience "emotional anesthesia" as a form of psychological self-protection. This is described as a diminished capacity to feel any kind of emotion, including those related to love and intimacy. It is easy to see how this disorder could be detrimental to a marriage or even a friendship.

Treatments for Anxiety Disorders

As with mood disorders, we advocate a three-fold approach to treatment of anxiety disorders: medication, psychotherapy and faith. Once again, before medication is even considered, a physician must first rule out any medical illness that might actually cause anxiety or anxiety-like symptoms. These include thyroid disease, hypoglycemia, mild head injury and (of course) menopause or premenstrual syndrome. There are also certain medications that can produce anxiety symptoms. These include steroids, certain asthma medications, certain decongestants and stimulants (which are usually prescribed to treat attention deficit disorder or obesity). If these medications need to be taken regularly, your physician can usually adjust the dosage to minimize any unpleasant anxious side effects.

Another culprit in the unnecessary production of anxiety symptoms is that most ubiquitous substance, caffeine. Most of us willingly consume this drug in one form or another. Believe it or not, the elimination of caffeine from the diet has been known to completely cure the symptoms of anxiety disorder in some people. (Be aware that sudden or rapid discontinuation of caffeine can cause "withdrawal symptoms" that also mimic anxiety.) However, the authors of this work would rather endure the symptoms of anxiety for the rest of their lives than give up even one cup of morning java, thank you very much.

Medications

Once a patient's diet and medical status has been assessed and accounted for, there are a number of medications on the market that can be used to help treat anxiety disorders successfully. Some of these must be taken every day, and some may be taken as needed, depending on the type of anxiety disorder that is being experienced. Unlike most of the antidepressants, there are some antianxiety medications that are highly addictive and must be administered and used with extreme caution (or not at all, if the person has a history of substance abuse). Here is a partial list of antianxiety—or "anxiolytic"—medications, grouped according to their use and addictive potential.

Anxiety Disorder	Medication Brand Name	Generic Name	Addictive Potential
Generalized Anxiety Disorder	BuSpar	buspirone	No
Panic Disorder	Xanax Klonopin	alprazolam clonazepam	Yes No
Other Anxiety Disorders	Valium Ativan	diazepam lorazepam	Yes Yes (with long-term use)

Psychotherapy

Psychotherapy is the next component of treatment for anxiety disorders. In therapy, the clinician often focuses on desensitizing the patient to anxiety-provoking situations, as previously described, or on helping the patient exert some intellectual or cognitive influence over his or her fearful reactions (referred to as "cognitive behavior modification"). These approaches are most effective for specific phobias or generalized anxiety disorder. However, extreme anxiety disorders like PTSD often require long-term therapy to deal with the traumatic event and its consequences. This is particularly difficult if the trauma was experienced repeatedly over time, as in some cases of physical or sexual abuse. In such cases, much work may be needed to help the individual acknowledge, confront and eventually forgive the offender. This is usually only a prelude to even more work on the self-esteem issues that inevitably accompany trauma or abuse. These issues are addressed in more detail later in this book.

The Good News

It has been our experience that committed Christians have the best prognosis for recovery from anxiety disorders because of their spiritual convictions and their constant attention to issues of faith. What hope is there for someone in the world who is unwilling or unable to turn to the living God and avail himself of the invitation to "Cast all your anxiety on him because he cares for you"? (1 Peter 5:7). How encouraging it is to treat disciples, who have the Holy Spirit as well as the blessings of devoted friends, to augment their treatment with medication and therapy. Although some disciples' struggles with anxiety remain lifelong, they can be victorious each and every day by the grace of God.

5

Psychotic Disorders

Depression and anxiety are, to some extent, a component of everyone's life. Therefore, they often go unidentified as disorders until it is obvious that they are being experienced in excess of the norm. Not so with psychotic disorders, the symptoms of which are more quickly and readily identified as "abnormal." The common element in all psychotic disorders is the presence of "psychosis," which is an inability to perceive or remain in contact with reality. Psychosis can take the form of hallucinations (seeing or hearing things which are not there), delusions (unrealistic or bizarre thoughts) or disturbed/disorganized thinking.

'Positive Symptoms'
Hallucinations most often involve the perception of voices, sounds or "visions" that may or may not be familiar to the individual. For example, the patient may hear—and hold conversations with—deceased loved ones or famous people from the past. They may actually see the person or entity to which they are speaking. They may also see other things such as ghosts, angels, demons or God. It's a good thing that psychologists didn't exist in the first century, as some of them might have turned a skeptical eye on the true, divinely created visions that

were necessary to convey God's word in the days before the Bible was available in its entirety!

The DSM-IV describes delusions as "erroneous beliefs that usually involve a misinterpretation of perceptions or experiences" (APA 1994, 275). For example, a person may think that he is being spied upon, followed or plotted against by individuals or groups of people whom he has never even met. This is referred to as a "paranoid" or "persecutory delusion." A person experiencing delusions of reference may hold the belief that certain sentences in books or the words or behaviors of others are specifically directed at him. There are also delusions of grandeur in which the person believes himself to be someone of incredible significance, such as an agent of God or the reincarnation of a famous historical figure. Finally, there are especially bizarre delusions involving the perception that one no longer has control of his own mind or body. Such persons may think that thoughts are being inserted into their heads, or that their actions are being manipulated by some outside agent or entity, such as another person or even an extraterrestrial being!

The disorganized thinking shown by psychotic patients is usually evident in the way that they communicate. Their speech usually skips quickly from one idea to another. These ideas may be only loosely related, or sometimes not related at all. Whereas even some "normal" people do this to some extent, the psychotic patient's inability to follow a single, logical train of thought makes him almost impossible to understand at times. These disorganized thoughts and speech patterns are among the defining characteristics of a psychotic disorder. Taken together, the symptoms of hallucinations, delusions and disorganized speech are known as the "positive symptoms" of a psychotic disorder.

'Negative Symptoms'

In addition to hallucinations, delusions and disturbed thought processes, the psychotic individual may also show a very narrow range of emotions at certain times ("affective flattening"). Even when talking about significant things, they may show little emotional expression in their facial expressions or tones of voice. They may actually avoid eye contact and show decreased speech production ("alogia"). They may also exhibit an inability to plan, initiate or persist in any kind of goal-directed activity ("avolition"). Taken together, these symptoms (affective flattening, alogia and avolition) are known as the "negative symptoms" of a psychotic disorder.

Types of Psychotic Disorders

The different types of psychotic disorders are generally classified by the length of time that the symptoms persist, as well as by the other symptoms that are present during the active phase of the illness. "Schizophrenia" is probably the most well known psychotic disorder (although it is often mistaken for "split personality," which is a completely different disorder.) It is a chronic illness that usually occurs in episodes. In other words, over the course of the person's life, periods of relatively normal functioning are interrupted by acute episodes of positive and/or negative symptoms. By definition, these acute episodes involve at least one month of uninterrupted positive symptoms. Such patients usually need to stay on medication their entire lives in order to prevent the recurrence of psychotic episodes. In contrast, there is also a disease known as "schizophreniform disorder" that involves only a single episode of psychosis that remits quickly and may never return. This is also sometimes known as a "brief psychotic reaction."

Finally, psychotic symptoms can sometimes occur in the context of a severe depression. When the symptoms of schizophrenia are interspersed with episodes of depression, the individual is said to be suffering from a "schizoaffective disorder." On the other hand, when the symptoms of depression predominate and are interspersed with occasional psychotic symptoms, the person is given a diagnosis of "major depression with psychotic features." In either case depressive and psychotic symptoms are usually treated simultaneously with a combination of antidepressant and antipsychotic medications.

Causes of Psychotic Disorders

Our understanding of the causes of psychotic disorders has grown substantially since the first medications for schizophrenia were developed in the 1950s. Interestingly, much like cancer, psychotic disorders appear to have a number of possible causes. It is known that overproduction of the neurotransmitter "dopamine" causes psychotic symptoms. This is the same neurochemical that is implicated in certain other neurological disorders, such as Parkinson's disease. The movie *Awakenings*, starring Robin Williams and Robert De Niro, is very instructive on the relationship between these two disorders. Most recently, schizophrenia has also been linked to abnormalities in the structure of the brain. It appears to have a very strong hereditary component, such that a person who has a schizophrenic family member is ten times more likely to have a psychotic disorder himself. Once again, a thorough investigation of an individual's family history is essential when a diagnosis of schizophrenia (or any of the other psychotic disorders) is considered.

Unlike some other psychiatric diseases, psychotic disorders rarely develop before early adulthood. In fact, the typical schizophrenic patient is usually in his middle to late twenties when he experiences his first psychotic episode. Consequently, this disorder has been known to devastate careers and marriages. One of us recalls a patient who was on his way to becoming a prominent vascular surgeon when he had his first psychotic episode while serving his hospital residency. We have both worked with children who have shown the first manifestations of a psychotic disorder at a very young age, but these cases are rare.

Medications

On the positive side, there are a number of "new and improved" antipsychotic medications on the market that have proven highly effective in the treatment of these disorders. Many of these newer medications have relatively few side effects and can enable the patient to live a normal life, as long as he or she is committed to sticking with treatment. Here is a list of some of the medications that are used to treat psychotic disorders:

Brand Name	Generic Name
Risperidal	risperidone
Thorazine	chlorpromazine
Clozaril	clozapine
Mellaril	thioridazine
Haldol	haloperidol
Loxitane	loxapine
Trilafon	perphenazine
Navane	thiothixine

This list is not exhaustive, primarily because new treatments are being added to the market on what seems to be an almost daily basis. It is encouraging that so much research time and money is being invested nationally in an attempt to find ever more effective treatments for these sometimes devastating disorders.

As always, before medication is even considered, it is important to rule out any other medical disorders that cause or mimic schizophrenic symptoms. These include (but are not limited to) systemic lupus erythematosis, vitamin B_{12} deficiency, multiple sclerosis, hypothyroidism and Alzheimer's disease. Furthermore, there are a number of drugs that can cause or induce a psychotic episode. These include illicit substances such as "crack" cocaine, LSD and psilocybin mushrooms. There are also "legitimate" medications that can cause psychosis, such as steroids, anti-Parkinsonian drugs and even some over-the-counter cold medications.

Helping Psychotic Patients

One might ask why we would devote an entire chapter to a group of disorders that occurs in only about one-half to one percent of the population (as opposed to, say, anywhere from five to twenty-five percent in the case of major depression). Even with such a low prevalence, one is bound to come across someone suffering from a psychotic disorder at some point in the course of trying to seek and save the lost. Many times our office has been called by well-meaning disciples who have begun to study the Bible with someone who reveals (if it is not readily evident) that they are being treated for schizophrenia. Quite frequently, the individual is not even sure what he or she is being treated for. In such cases the disciple will call with the name of the person's prescription drug and ask us to "work backward" in an effort to identify the exact illness.[1]

Even though there is no direct correlation between psychosis and intelligence (in fact, some persons suffering from psychotic disorders are highly intelligent), disciples who study with one of these patients may question the person's ability to interpret and understand spiritual and Biblical principles. This is a legitimate concern since psychotic patients, even while on medication, sometimes struggle with keeping their thoughts organized or with holding onto the distinction between delusion and reality. Some patients actually suffer from delusions that have religious themes. For example, they feel that they are an agent of God or the direct recipient of some godly revelation. In such cases Bible study may need to be deferred

[1]Lists of medications are provided throughout this book so that you can do the same thing.

until the person has become more stable through psychiatric treatment. The well-meaning disciple can help these people the most by ensuring that they find appropriate help, keep up with treatment and continue to take their medications on a regular basis. On an encouraging note, we know of several people suffering from chronic or lifelong psychotic disorders who have—with the help and support of friends and family— become productive and fruitful disciples themselves.

6

Personality Disorders

As mentioned earlier, there is a group of disorders that is felt to be caused not by chemical imbalances or malformations in the brain, but by disturbances in early psychological or emotional development. These disorders, known as personality disorders, are caused by the development of unfavorable personality traits that interfere with an individual's ability to relate to or think about himself and his environment. These are true character problems that become sufficiently severe as to impede the formation of "normal" relationships with others.

Of course, every human being on earth has flaws in his character. Anyone who has ever studied the Bible in earnest knows that we all "fall short of the glory of God" because of these imperfections (Romans 3:23). It can probably be said that in God's eyes we *all* have a personality problem! However, most of us are able to make a sincere effort to conquer our character weaknesses once we come to conviction about God's grace and the need to obey his word. In contrast, the character problems in persons with personality disorders are inflexible and enduring. They cannot be accounted for solely by stubbornness or hard-heartedness. Even by the world's standards, these people cannot live a normal life because of the severity of their maladaptive or unusual personality traits.

The First Cluster of Disorders

The DSM-IV divides the personality disorders into three main groups or "clusters." People with disorders in the first cluster have personality traits that make them appear odd or eccentric. For example, individuals with schizoid personality disorder are usually uninterested in or uncomfortable with social relationships of any type. They are reclusive individuals who appear cold, detached and aloof. They show little or no emotion and are indifferent to both praise and criticism. In addition to this reduced capacity for social relationships, people with schizotypal personality disorder have odd or "magical" beliefs that set them apart from others. Someone with this disorder may, for example, claim to have "special powers," such as the ability to control others or foresee events before they happen. Of course, such disorders must be placed in the context of the person's culture: A shaman or medicine man in a society in Central Asia who claims to use clairvoyant powers to locate food would, for example, not qualify for a diagnosis of schizotypal personality.

The Second Cluster of Disorders

The second cluster of personality disorders involves personality traits that cause a person to appear dramatic, emotional or erratic. The most insidious of these is probably antisocial personality disorder, in which the individual shows a habitual disregard for rules, laws and the rights or feelings of others. This is the so-called psychopath or sociopath who has been artistically portrayed in such movies as *Silence of the Lambs* and *Clockwork Orange*. Our most famous modern-day, real-life serial killers probably suffer from this disorder. However, individuals with antisocial personality can also appear "smooth," caring and socially adept. In the end it is invariably discovered that their interest in others was never sincere but only a ruse to achieve some selfish goal. We know of more than one person like this who has actually been studied with and baptized. Only later did we find out that they were "wolves in sheep's clothing" (Matthew 7:15) who sought only to use the body of Christ to achieve some self-serving end.

Somewhat more common but less easy to detect are other disorders in the second personality disorder cluster. These include histrionic personality disorder, in which the individual engages in extreme emotionality and attention-seeking behavior. This disorder, which is (perhaps surprisingly) equally prevalent in women and men, is characterized by theatrical behaviors and a need to always be "the life of the party." Such persons usually make an excellent first impression because they are bubbly, outgoing, lively, ingratiating, flattering and charming. Often they are sexually seductive or flirtatious. However, it is quickly discovered that they are capable of maintaining only superficial relationships that lack any real depth or intimacy. Their emotions are shallow and often change quickly. Consequently, their friendships with others rarely endure.

The term "narcissistic personality disorder" is applied to people who perceive themselves as "special" and deserving of excessive admiration. These are self-important people who seem to feel entitled to special treatment. They may be preoccupied with fantasies of unlimited wealth or power. As might be expected, they also lack empathy and are unwilling to recognize the needs of others. This disorder embodies the sins of selfishness, arrogance and self-love. Once again, to be considered part of a disorder, these sins should be seen in excess of the "typical" hard-heartedness of people in the world. Persons with narcissistic personality disorder are likely to be unwilling to acknowledge their deficiencies and to recognize their need to repent.

The Third Cluster of Disorders

The final diagnosis in this cluster is perhaps the most perplexing and frustrating to deal with. This diagnosis, termed "borderline personality disorder," is described in the DSM-IV as "...a pervasive pattern of instability of interpersonal relationships, self-image, and affects, and marked impulsivity that begins by early adulthood and is present in a variety of contexts" (APA 1994, 650). In almost plain English, individuals with this disorder are emotionally unstable people who show extreme mood swings and impulsive behaviors in reaction to their tumultuous relationships with others. As a group these people are extremely dependent and fearful of rejection or abandonment. They constantly seek reassurance, approval and verification that they are loved and cared about. In this context, they interpret every change in plan or unkept promise as proof that they are "bad" and have been abandoned.

For example, they may become furious or frantic when someone is late for a date, even if there is a justifiable cause or reason. In turn, the patient then retaliates by engaging in some extremely impulsive, usually self-destructive behavior such as self-mutilation or a suicide attempt. It is usually hoped that this action will fill the "offender" with guilt, remorse or the strong desire to return and care for them forever. As you can imagine, persons with borderline personality disorder often experience "dramatic shifts in their views of others" (APA 1994, 651). Their feelings for another person may switch abruptly from adoration to disdain in response to a perceived rejection. The character played by Glen Close in the movie *Fatal Attraction* might be the best example here. Interestingly, the vast majority (about seventy-five percent) of people with this disorder are women. Why? The authors of this book choose to defer this question in the interest of preserving marital harmony.

The final cluster of personality disorders entails counterproductive personality traits that make a person appear unusually anxious or timid. For instance, people with "avoidant personality disorder" tend to be excessively fearful of criticism and disapproval. Consequently, they avoid work, school or social activities that would place them in any kind of position to be evaluated by others. This disorder often starts in childhood in the form of excessive shyness or fearfulness of new situations. The second disorder in this cluster, called "dependent personality disorder," is characterized by "...an excessive need to be taken care of that leads to submissive and clinging behavior and fears of separation" (APA 1994, 665). These people have difficulty making even simple everyday decisions because of their constant need for advice and reassurance. This appears to be the antithesis of the sin of pride

The last disorder in this cluster that bears discussion is "obsessive-compulsive personality disorder." This is an entity that is completely different from the more familiar obsessive-compulsive disorder, which is an Axis I disorder in which the person experiences a compulsive need to engage in a repetitive behavior (such as hand-washing, counting or checking) in response to a disturbing obsessive thought (such as worry about becoming contaminated with germs every time something is touched). Obsessive-compulsive disorder is actually an anxiety disorder that can be treated with certain psychoactive medications.

In contrast, the obsessive-compulsive personality disorder is characterized by an excessive preoccupation with orderliness, rules or details. People with this disorder are perfectionists who often sacrifice time and efficiency in the interest of meticulousness, organization and proper protocol. These individuals are decidedly no fun to be with. They rarely take time out for relaxation because they see this as a waste of time. Like Ebenezer Scrooge, they are miserly, stingy and rigid when it comes to issues of ethics or principle. They are legalistic individuals who expect total compliance to rules, without excuse or exception. Jesus probably encountered many Pharisees in his day that might have been worthy of this diagnosis. In fact, in our own century, many of our own fathers who grew up during the Great Depression (historical, not emotional) were raised to have some of the characteristics of an obsessive-compulsive personality. Indeed, this disorder is about twice as prevalent in men as in women. Husbands with this disorder are described as extremely difficult to live with, unless of course they were lucky enough to marry a woman with dependent personality disorder![1]

With God's Help

As you read this section on personality disorders, you were probably able to think of at least one friend, acquaintance or family member who fits each description perfectly. Isn't it interesting that we all have some of the characteristics of each of these disorders? When it all comes down to it, these personality disorders are merely amplifications of the sinful nature that is common to all men and women, as discussed in the seventh and eighth chapters of Romans. However, persons with personality disorders may find it exceptionally difficult to gain this spiritual perspective. They may be completely comfortable with the way they are and find the notion that they have a "problem" completely ludicrous. This is partly why these people are so difficult to treat and even more difficult to convert to Christianity! Even more so than the "normal" person, it may be exceptionally difficult to help them see their sinfulness and convince them of their need to repent in order to avail themselves of God's grace. However, as Jesus said in Matthew 19:26, "With man this is impossible, but with God all things are possible." With time and enormous patience on the part of those who are committed to help them, we have actually seen people virtually "cured" of personality disorders, to the amazement and consternation of their psychiatrists!

Once again, a good rule of thumb is to steer the person toward treatment with the right kind of mental health professional and help them remain in treatment as you deal with

[1]See our earlier comments in Chapter 2 regarding Axis II disorders and their treatment.

their spiritual needs. Now that we have looked at a wide range of psychiatric and emotional challenges we are ready to look at the different types of help that are available in the world of mental health professionals.

7

Treatment Issues

As part of the three-fold approach to psychiatric problems we described earlier, some disciples need the help of a psychotherapist or professional counselor. Although the Bible says that we are all "competent to counsel" (Romans 15:14), special expertise is often needed to help deal with a specific psychiatric disorder that exceeds the limitations of "typical" discipling or shepherding. Much like that of the discipling partner, the role of the therapist is to help the patient learn how to deal with stressful events that exacerbate or contribute to the psychiatric disorder. A discipler does this by putting those events in the context of faith and spiritual health. Therapists, on the other hand, have been trained in special techniques to help patients change their way of thinking in order to conquer the self-defeating, unrealistic or unproductive thoughts that are *specific to a particular disorder.* They have received specialized training in the diagnosis and treatment of depression, anxiety disorders, eating disorders and any number of other problems that have biological and psychological (not just spiritual) components.

But how does one choose an appropriate therapist? How can the techniques of psychotherapy be reconciled with Christian faith? Does everyone need therapy? Once treatment has started, what are the important things to look out for? These are the questions that we will attempt to answer in this chapter.

Choosing a Therapist

> *Question:* "What is the difference between a psychiatrist and a psychologist?"
>
> *Answer:* "About forty bucks an hour."

This joke (which we've actually told to patients in response to their questions about "shrinks") humorously illustrates the bewildering array of mental health professionals. Each has his or her own approach to dealing with psychiatric disorders, depending on how—and to what level—the therapist has been trained. However, before we try to sort through the various types of mental health providers, we must first deal with the issue of therapy from a Christian perspective.

In order to deal with the emotional problems that contribute to a mental disorder, one must be prepared to divulge and discuss some intimately personal details about self and family. Disciples are usually good at this. Based on their convictions about the Bible, true disciples have agreed to be open with their lives and to share such details with other people of like conviction, in the interest of confessing sin which brings healing (James 5:16). In other words, disciples are no strangers to sharing sensitive information with one another.

However, it is understandable that disciples may be hesitant to share this kind of information with people "in the world," even trained mental health professionals. Will the clinician in the world be respectful of the disciple's convictions about the Bible? Will the clinician be able to recognize sin in the disciple's life and take a stand against it, rather than excuse it as a symptom—or even consider it as something "normal"? It is because of such issues that disciples prefer to see other disciples when therapy is called for. Alas, there are not nearly enough mental health professionals in the kingdom to go around! Therefore one must actually seek help in the world on occasion. We have encouraged many Christians who live elsewhere but seek our advice on a particular psychiatric problem to find a therapist who will be able to deal competently with that particular problem.

To that end, we urge you to be an informed consumer and to understand your rights as part of the therapeutic relationship. Virtually all of the mental health professions, such as psychiatry and psychology, have their own codes of ethics, devised and published by their own professional organizations. These codes differ somewhat from profession to profession and sometimes from state to state. However, almost every code includes a principle that prohibits the clinician from influencing the beliefs and values of the patient in any way. In other words, it would be unethical for any therapist to try to influence or change a patient's religious or spiritual convictions, no matter what they are.

Were a patient to come to our office who believed in sacrificing household pets to some pagan god, it would be unethical for us to try to change that belief, even if that belief were distasteful to us personally. According to the ethical code of the American Psychological Association, if a patient's belief system is so personally offensive to us as to interfere with effective, unbiased counseling, then we must make this known to the patient and refer the patient on to someone else.

Most mental health professions require training in these ethical principles before a clinician can be licensed. In other words, even "worldly" therapists have been told that they must be respectful of your belief in the Bible and your outlook on faith, sin and God *as long as you make these beliefs known to them from the outset.* It has occurred to us that disciples have a conflict of beliefs with their therapists only when they do not tell the therapist what those beliefs are. Therefore, before you choose a therapist, and certainly before you enter into the highly personal relationship of patient and therapist, *ask* the therapist what his or her views are about spirituality and the Bible. If you sense that you will not be able to work with this person, go elsewhere. Would you not do that with a pediatrician or family physician? Remember that you are the consumer.

When it comes down to it, a patient will only be able to work well with a clinician with whom he or she can build a trusting relationship. A clinician who is warm, caring, sensitive and empathetic will engender such trust. We believe that you will know within five minutes of your first phone contact or face-to-face visit whether or not a clinician possesses these qualities. However, these qualities alone are insufficient. (If this were not the case, most patients would be able to save lots of money by talking to their mother rather than a therapist.) The clinician must also be trusted to have sufficient knowledge and training to be able to help with the problem. This can usually be determined by the letters after their name.

When mental health professionals are sorted out strictly by level of education, two categories emerge: doctoral and nondoctoral. Doctoral-level clinicians are those who have received a "terminal degree," i.e. the highest degree that our educational system can offer. Among these professionals are *psychiatrists*, all of whom are physicians who have been specially trained to recognize and treat mental disorders. Psychiatrists have graduated from medical school and have been trained to administer medicine and to deal with the physical components of a mental disorder. Most have also been trained to do therapy, but over the years this profession has narrowed its focus somewhat to include mostly the prescription, monitoring and management of medication. Nowadays it is common for a psychiatrist to manage the medication component of patient care, while a psychologist or other therapist conducts the counseling. This approach may seem unnecessarily inconvenient for the patient at times. However, the team approach has the advantage of ensuring that at least two professional minds are being applied to the care of one patient. It allows for a checks and balances system wherein two different professions bring their unique but complementary skills to bear on the same problem. In addition, it is sometimes a less expensive approach, since it allows the psychiatrist (usually the most expensive player on the team) to see the patient less frequently. In any event a psychiatrist will either be an M.D. (Medical Doctor) or D.O. (Doctor of Osteopathy). *Psychologists* constitute the other group of doctoral-level clinicians. Psychologists have not been to medical school and therefore, are not allowed to prescribe medication. However, they have been to graduate school and have earned one of the following terminal degrees:

- Ph.D. (Doctor of Philosophy)
- Psy.D. (Doctor of Psychology)
- Ed.D. (Doctor of Education)

Psychologists are similar to psychiatrists in that they have received specialized training in the diagnosis and treatment of mental disorders. In addition, clinical psychologists have learned how to administer and interpret psychological tests, determining such things as a patient's level of intelligence (IQ testing) and his current emotional state (using instruments such as the famous Rorschach Inkblot Test). The ability to administer psychological tests is unique to this profession. As noted earlier, this kind of testing is integral to the process of correctly diagnosing a mental disorder. In fact certain disorders, such as learning disabilities and mental retardation, can only be diagnosed with the help of psychological testing.

During training, psychologists learn the clinical practice of analyzing and influencing human behavior. They also learn how to do therapy, usually by participating in practical learning situations like internships. There are a number of different approaches to therapy, from the extremely practical ("reality therapy" for example) to the more, shall we say, nontraditional and rarely used (for instance, "primal scream therapy"). Some approaches are more applicable to certain disorders than others. Once again, before therapy even starts, it would be wise to inquire as to what approach the therapist will use and why.

There is a myriad of mental health professions at the nondoctoral level. Most of these practitioners have earned advanced degrees (such as a master's degree) in various disciplines and have subsequently received special training in the therapeutic treatment of mental disorders. Here are a few of the titles by which these professionals are recognized:

- LMFT (Licensed Marriage and Family Therapist)
- LCSW (Licensed Clinical Social Worker)
- LPC (Licensed Professional Counselor)
- PNP (Psychiatric Nurse Practitioner)
- CAC (Certified Addiction Counselor)

Notice that these acronyms are not educational degrees. They refer to the specialized certification that has been awarded to the master's-level professional. Each of these certifications entitles the professional to do a particular kind of therapy. However, none can prescribe medication. Therefore, like psychologists, they frequently have to arrange for the patient to see a psychiatrist or physician if they think that medication might be required. Public mental health centers, psychiatric hospitals and larger private practices often treat patients in teams consisting of physicians, psychologists and/or master's-level counselors.

Master's-level mental health professionals engage mostly in "talking therapy," or counseling. The approach they use depends on how they have been trained and the nature of the special population that they usually treat. Certified addiction counselors, for example, specialize in helping addicts overcome their addictions. Licensed marriage and family therapists specialize in just that: helping families and marriages work better. If you are not sure what kind of counselor or mental health professional is best able to help you, asking your family physician is a good place to start. With just a little information about your problem, he or she may be in the best position to refer you to the appropriate professional in your area. Many insurance companies now require a referral directly from your so-called "primary care physician" (PCP) anyway.

In addition to lots of training, education, warmth and empathy, there is one more quality that you should expect of a prospective therapist or other mental health professional: a license. Each state in the union has established a set of minimal standards for each type of clinician to meet before he or she can be allowed to practice independently in that state. Before being licensed to practice, each clinician must submit his educational records for review by a state board and in most cases, pass some kind of state or national test to demonstrate competency. Interestingly, the states vary in what they consider competent. For example, in a few states clinicians can call themselves "psychologists" with only master's degrees. In most other states, however, this title can only be used by people with doctoral degrees.

The point is this—don't see anyone who has not been licensed by the state to practice his or her profession. The degree that someone earns in school and the amount of training her or she has is pretty much meaningless unless that person has obtained the state's seal of approval to practice. Without exception, it is unlawful to practice any of the professions listed above in any state without a license. You may find people who have an office and some kind of fancy title, but unless they have a license, they are not psychiatrists, psychologists, social workers or professional counselors. Let the buyer beware!

Financial Concerns

Let's say that you have developed some convictions about needing to see a mental health professional, and you have some understanding of what kind of professional you need to see. Now, how are you going to pay for it?

Most mental health professionals in private practice are, by most people's standards, expensive. Therefore, very few patients can pay for these services out-of-pocket. This is the purpose of medical insurance. However, keep in mind that not all insurance policies cover mental health services in the same way that they cover strictly medical services. Our advice: Do not even walk into a clinician's office until you have called your insurance company and asked exactly how (and how much) they pay for—to use insurance language—"nervous and mental conditions." Unfortunately, they may need to ask you some nosey and personal questions about your suspected "condition" before they can answer that question. Under the relatively new "managed care system" of health insurance coverage, your insurance company may then limit the types of clinicians they will pay for you to see.

For example, some insurance companies will pay for part of your visit to a psychiatrist, but they will pay proportionally more for a visit to a master's-level counselor because his or her rates are lower, costing the company less. The company may also pay for you to see a clinician the first time and then negotiate with the clinician for a subsequent number of visits based on need. Certain policies may pay for some diagnoses, such as major depression, but not for others, such as a personality disorder. Similarly, they may pay for some services, such as therapy, but not others, such as psychological testing. Once again, the best idea is to be a wise consumer and to contact your insurance company before you consult a mental health clinician for the first time.

What if you do not have insurance? Fortunately, there are a few practitioners who will actually adjust their fees based on the income of the patient (the so-called "sliding fee scale"). In addition, all states provide some way to care for persons who need counseling or psychiatric care but cannot afford it. These usually take the form of community-based mental health centers that provide a wide range of outpatient psychiatric, counseling and substance abuse treatment services. In addition they are commonly affiliated with state-run psychiatric hospitals where patients can be admitted if they require inpatient care. Local mental health centers can usually be found in the phone book under state or county government listings.

Staying Compliant with Treatment

In 2 Kings 5:1-15 we are told the story of Naaman, a great commander in the army of the King of Aram. Naaman had a disorder for which he was willing to seek treatment. He was referred to Elisha, a "doctor" who obviously had a good reputation for curing diseases. Evidently, the Aramean army had excellent health benefits, and so Naaman was able to go to his first appointment loaded with money and ready to pay for the best of care.

Naaman certainly had his own expectations for what would happen during his treatment. When his first visit failed to meet his expectations, he was indignant! He felt that Elisha had not given him the personal attention to which he was entitled. Furthermore, he had a real problem with Elisha's prescription: it was his learned opinion that the medications in Damascus were far superior to those in Israel! Only after he humbled himself and submitted himself completely to treatment did Naaman recover.

The story of Naaman puts us in mind of many Christians who have tried to seek psychiatric help. It is understandably unnerving for disciples to have to seek therapy and to entrust the therapist with intimate details about their emotional problems. Consequently, disciples often respond to "worldly" treatment with doubt and distrust. They may be quick to find reasons not to comply with the therapist's recommendations. However, it is interesting to note that most disciples would be far quicker to trust a surgeon to put them to sleep and cut them with a knife—a procedure that is much more potentially hazardous than psychotherapy—because it is more or less what they expect medical treatment to be like. Just as in Naaman's case, it all comes down to the issues of trust and faith.

Psalm 91 tells us that the Lord will always protect those who call upon his name. It is easy to see from the Old Testament that God uses worldly agents—kings, armies and entire nations—to help his people. When someone we love is in the hospital, we pray daily that God will be with the doctors and nurses and that he will work through them to effect a cure. The same principle applies to the world of mental health: Yes, make a wise choice about where and how to seek treatment, but then trust that God will use the doctor or therapist to work "for the good of those who love him, who have been called according to his purpose" (Romans 8:28).

The tendency to distrust treatment in the world usually leads to a particular problem that seems to be characteristic of Christians: premature discontinuation of treatment when the patient feels that no progress is being made or that progress is too slow. For example the patient has been in therapy or on a medication for three whole days (or weeks or months) and still feels the same. At this point the *polite* (not to be confused with righteous) patient will come in for a visit, assure the clinician that he or she feels much better, thank the clinician for everything, pay off the bill (hopefully) and never be heard from again. The *impolite* patient, on the other hand, just stops showing up for visits. This places the clinician in a very uncomfortable position, since the clinician is still ethically responsible for the patient until the doctor-patient relationship has been formally terminated in some way.

Our advice here is to be a *patient* patient. Naaman was told by Elisha to wash in the Jordan seven times: not six, and not one—either of which would have been quicker and more convenient—but seven. Elisha had his reasons for this, which were not readily evident to Naaman. Naaman had only to trust that Elisha knew exactly how long this treatment would take.

Unfortunately, treatment of emotional problems is not an exact science. No doctor or therapist can say with Elisha's confidence how long someone may need to remain in treatment. Medications, for example, work differently in different individuals, depending on factors like weight and metabolism. Therefore, either dosages need to be adjusted or different medications need to be tried before a satisfactory medicine is found. The patient must resist the temptation to adjust or discontinue his or her own medication because results are not coming quickly enough. Interestingly, many patients respond quickly to medication and notice a great deal of improvement almost immediately. Such patients are often tempted to think that they have been "cured" and no longer have to take their medication! Therefore, they face the same temptation to discontinue treatment before it is wise to do so.

Predicting progress in therapy is difficult, despite the fact that clinicians are now frequently asked to do so by their patients' insurance companies. However, most responsible clinicians maintain some sort of treatment plan for each patient, consisting of notes about the patient's progress, goals for therapy and estimates about the time that it will take to achieve each goal. This treatment plan is usually reviewed regularly with the patient. If not, the patient needs to feel free to ask about his or her treatment plan. Every patient is entitled to this information, which is held to the ethical standard of "confidentiality." In other words, it (as well as all information about a patient's diagnosis and history) cannot be shared with any other party without the written permission of the patient.

Trusting God in Treatment

In sum, Jesus admonished his disciples to be "shrewd as snakes and as innocent as doves" (Matthew 10:16). Therefore, the Christian seeking treatment for a psychiatric or emotional problem is obliged to be a wise consumer who makes informed decisions about the quality of the treatment he or she is to receive. Of course, because of the weakened condition one is in when needing such help, it is wise to have faithful and mature disciples to give advice as these decisions are made.

We hope that the information in this chapter will prove useful in making a choice about a therapist. However, once a course of treatment has been chosen, trust that God will use doctors, therapists and medication in such a way that "no harm will befall you, no disaster will come near your tent. For he will command his angels concerning you to guard you in all your ways" (Psalm 91:10-11).

8

Helping Disciples Face Emotional Challenges: A Guide for Ministry Leaders and Friends

Until now you may have been reading about the emotional struggles of others with dispassionate interest, grateful to God that you have never had to deal personally with any of the psychiatric troubles discussed in previous chapters. However, if you are a disciple, the Bible calls you to be empathetic and to encourage the weak (see, for example, 1 Thessalonians 5:14, Galatians 6:2, and 2 Corinthians 11:29), because we are all weak in one way or another. As one who has taken up this charge, you will invariably come across someone who has struggled or is struggling with a psychiatric problem, one which exceeds your counseling experience and makes you feel "in over your head." What can you, as a church leader, or merely a Christian who is trying to compassionately guide a brother or sister, do to help? Jesus taught in parables, so maybe we should try to answer this question with a story.

The Parable of Mark and Joe

Mark had been discipling Joe, a fairly new Christian, for only a few months when Joe was involved in a serious car accident. In addition to many cuts and contusions, Joe also suffered a broken leg that his doctors thought might take up to six months to heal. Thankfully, the doctors told Joe that if he was careful, followed their advice and saw a physical therapist, he would probably make a complete recovery.

Mark was very concerned about Joe's physical health, of course, but he was also concerned about Joe's spiritual health during this recovery time. He wanted Joe not only to stay faithful, but also to grow spiritually during this trying period. So Mark visited Joe in the hospital as soon as he could receive visitors, taking him his Bible and some great DPI books that he thought might encourage him (for example, *This Doesn't Feel Like Love* by Roger and Marsha Lamb and *Mind Change* by Thomas Jones). Of course, Joe was still in a lot of pain and on some fairly powerful analgesic medications, so Mark wisely made the visit short and encouraging, waiting until Joe would be feeling better before discussing "deep" spiritual issues.

Joe was discharged on a Saturday afternoon, and actually called Mark to see what he thought about Joe's coming to church the next morning. After getting advice, Mark called Joe back and suggested that it would probably be better for him to rest and recover a bit more. Instead, Mark set a time to get with Joe later in the afternoon to read the Bible, pray and bring him communion. He also planned to bring Joe a tape of the sermon so Joe could stay in step with the rest of the church and remain spiritually focused.

Joe seemed to do very well his first week out of the hospital. He called Mark daily to update him on his progress. Mark's Bible discussion group had planned a picnic and volleyball game at the end of the week to reach out to new people. Of course Mark knew that this kind of activity was too much for Joe, so he helped Joe make a plan to call three friends during the week and invite them to church.

The next week, Joe did terribly. He became impatient and decided it was time to "be well," ready or not. He did not get any advice about how to plan his week. As soon as he thought he was able, he went back to all of his old activities, including attending church twice a week, because he was just tired of being sick. Without telling anyone, he also stopped taking an antibiotic that the doctor had prescribed to prevent infection, stating that this medication made him feel weird. He also stopped going to the physical therapist because he felt it was not helping him. Consequently, he got so sick and worn out that he ended up missing church completely the following Sunday. When Mark called him on Sunday afternoon to find out what had happened, Joe sounded angry and frustrated. He told Mark that he probably would not be back at church for a while because he just could not keep up with all of the demands. Besides, Joe felt that he could not be an effective disciple with his injury, so he might as well stop trying, at least for right now.

Mark had a long talk with Joe on the phone, trying to help him refocus. First, he reminded Joe that this was a temporary situation, while his commitment to Jesus was permanent. He talked with Joe about other disciples who had remained faithful through similar trials. He also asked Joe if he had been reading and praying (which he had not) and helped Joe make a schedule of encouraging scriptures to focus on during the coming week.

Mark also gently rebuked Joe for not getting more advice. However, the rebuke was much less gentle when he found out that Joe had also stopped the recommended therapy and medication. Mark advised Joe to call his doctor immediately to find out how to get back on his recovery program and told Joe that he would help him keep faithful with the program by asking him about it more frequently. He could tell that Joe was faithless and discouraged at this point. Finally, Mark encouraged him to persevere and to continue to pray for complete recovery. He reminded Joe that this process might be slow and painful, but that he had God and the church to help him through. Mark himself prayed every day for Joe's complete recovery.

Joe's recovery was long, in fact several months longer than the doctors had first anticipated. Mark was a faithful friend to Joe throughout this time, encouraging him when he got discouraged and rebuking him when he got lazy, self-focused or faithless. Joe had to seek a lot of advice from older Christians and fellow disciples who had been through similar situations. Mark himself sometimes had to be rebuked about his own laziness and selfishness when it came to helping Joe. Through it all, both Mark and Joe learned many lessons about God, themselves and the kingdom; and both were later able to help others who encountered similar trials.

The Explanation

Hopefully, as you read through this illustration, you developed some appreciation for how difficult this time was for these disciples, both for the one who was ill and the one trying to help him. We generally seem to do better at "carrying each other's burdens" when the burden is a visible, physical illness: We cook meals, visit at the hospital and do whatever else we can think of to help and encourage the sick disciple. We tend to not be as helpful when one of our brothers or sisters is grappling with an emotional problem, usually because we are at a loss for what to do. Disciples typically feel helpless when it comes to a brother or sister who has been hospitalized, put on medication or referred for therapy due to emotional or mental challenges.

However, we need to care for the person suffering from an emotional illness in much the same way as we care for a person who is suffering from a physical illness. In other words, do not try to function as a doctor or therapist. Instead, function as a brother or a sister who loves the emotionally challenged disciple and wants to help that disciple get to heaven, regardless of the trials and challenges he or she may be facing. To this end, we offer the following suggestions that we hope will prove helpful to leaders and discipling partners in the kingdom.

Learning to Listen

As disciples, we often feel like we need to have a handy answer or a piece of advice for any and every situation. In working with people who are facing serious emotional challenges, one quickly learns that there are not any easy answers or solutions to the complicated problems they are facing. Therefore, it is often true (even for mental health professionals) that listening is the most appropriate help we can offer. Encourage the person to be honest about what he or she is thinking and feeling and to talk about his or her fears, hopes and feelings of hopelessness. This can be a great opportunity for you to share your own faith with someone during a faithless time (Philemon 4-7).

One word of caution here—don't be judgmental or easily shocked by what you hear. Many people suffering from depression or a thought disorder, or even obsessive-compulsive tendencies, may have thoughts and feelings that seem weird, even to them. (Remember, this is why these illnesses are called emotional "disorders"!) For instance, it is not at all unusual for a person with severe depression to struggle with suicidal thinking. This is a common symptom of major depression, and even strong Christians experience it—we will discuss this is greater detail later. Similarly, people with obsessive-compulsive disorder often exhibit thoughts and behaviors that they realize are bizarre, such as unrealistic fears about hurting a loved one or compulsively performing a ritualized behavior over and over. Knowing that these thoughts or behaviors are wrong, these Christians often will not share their struggles unless specifically asked. However, like all of us, what they really need is for another disciple to know about these struggles and to pray for them (James 5:16). Therefore, try to make it easy for them to share these feelings with you.

Learn to ask specific questions. Asking "How are you?" will probably be met with the obligatory "Just fine," or "Better, thank you." Instead, do not be afraid to ask more pointed questions such as: "How is your depression?" "Are you having any suicidal thoughts?" and "In what ways do you feel like you are doing better?" Be specific and help the struggling disciple to see that talking about serious subjects will not scare you off.

Usually when we see disciples in therapy, we recommend that they tell at least one or two other members of their congregation about what they are talking about in therapy. This is especially important if the disciple is seeing a non-Christian therapist. Remember that it is not your job to be a therapist to your brother or sister in Christ. However, you can certainly help the person stay spiritual through a difficult time.

Helping the Disciple Stay Close to God

One of the worst symptoms of depression is a feeling of emotional numbness. Many people who are depressed will say that, between periods of depression and hopelessness, they feel nothing—no joy, no love, no excitement, no pleasure. Even things that they once found enjoyment in no longer bring any good feelings. This is a symptomatic condition called "anhedonia," which some people find even more painful than tearfulness or despair. To make matters worse, people experiencing anhedonia usually find it hard to believe that they will ever feel differently. They resign themselves to it because they think it will last forever.

The symptoms of depression—anhedonia, impaired concentration and feelings of hopelessness and worthlessness—make it difficult for depressed Christians to maintain a close relationship with God. Whereas they once felt deep love and joy and excitement in their relationship with the Lord, now there is little or no feeling whatsoever. In addition, many of them struggle with intense feelings of insecurity and doubt that God even wants to have a relationship with them anymore. Of course, Satan is an expert at capitalizing on these feelings and will invariably take the opportunity to convince the disciple that it is time to give up. Many people stop praying or reading their Bible during these times, or they will only focus on scriptures that confirm their feelings of worthlessness and despair (for example, Isaiah 64:6 and Romans 3:12).

The same is often true of their time in fellowship. Whereas depressed Christians once felt excited to be with other disciples and enjoyed the activities of the kingdom, they now feel physically and emotionally exhausted. Participation in the body of Christ brings no joy. However, knowing that we are commanded to rejoice always, the disciples in turn feel guilty and afraid to confess their feelings to anyone. People who are depressed just want to go home, take the phone off the hook and go to bed for the rest of the day. Social isolation and inactivity appear very attractive, but only serve to make the depression worse.

During these times we have to help our struggling brothers and sisters to live out their commitment to God. When we become Christians, we make the decision to let our actions be dictated by God's word rather than by our feelings. However, it is easy to be misled by our feelings when they become so intense as to be virtually incapacitating. Consequently, we must remind our struggling friends that their commitment to God cannot be dependent on their unreliable emotions at any given time. We must encourage them to remain faithful to God and to fulfill their promises to him, even during periods of profound hopelessness and despair.

Studying

One of the easiest ways to do this is to encourage our friends to remain consistent in their Bible study. If decreased concentration is a problem, help the struggling disciple to focus on only one or two passages (rather than an entire chapter or book) and think about how to put those passages into action. We frequently encourage disciples who are having difficulty with attention and concentration to simply write out a verse or two on an index card and read it several times throughout the day. We try to help them find scriptures that are encouraging and meet their needs, especially those verses that combat (rather than promote) feelings of hopelessness and worthlessness. Some of these are included in our Bible studies in the last chapter of this book.

Christians who are struggling with emotional problems often state that reading and praying makes them feel like hypocrites, because there is so little feeling behind their actions. Again, it is useful to help them focus on honoring God with their actions by doing the right thing, regardless of how they are feeling. It helps if they can view their emotions as temporarily "broken" or "out of order," and therefore unreliable for the time being. One cannot rely on a broken leg during a marathon race. Similarly, the struggling disciple cannot rely on "broken" feelings to make spiritual decisions.

Praying

Depressed or emotionally challenged Christians need to be encouraged to talk honestly with God, sharing with him all of their doubts, fears and anxieties. This is a time to "get real" with God, even though this may feel very awkward or even embarrassing in the context of a depressed episode. In fact, disciples who are depressed usually stop praying altogether, or they pray very superficial prayers that only make them feel more disconnected with the Father. Remind them that God loves them like a father and wants to be with them during this difficult time. You may need to pray with the person for some time if he or she is extremely depressed and despondent.

Make sure to encourage the person to pray for a complete recovery from his or her illness. Although this seems rather basic, the thought of a complete recovery may seem totally beyond the despondent disciple. Again, you must understand how intense the feelings of hopelessness and despair can be during periods of clinical depression. If the person does not expect to get better, he or she may not even think of praying about it. Therefore, it is incumbent upon the leader or discipling partner to pray for the disciple's full recovery and to help the disciple pray for recovery as well.

Fellowship

Of course, there is no excuse for not praying or spending time in God's word, even for disciples who are facing emotional challenges. We have visited disciples in the hospital who have asked us to study and pray with them right there on the hospital unit, and those disciples are still faithful today. Do everything you can to help such disciples remain faithful in their commitment to God. In the same way they must be encouraged to stay close to other Christians and discouraged from being away from the church. Some people find it very difficult to be around crowds of people if they are depressed or anxious, and they will avoid church because of this. Encourage them to sit in the back if necessary (you may want to sit with them) and to talk to at least a few people in fellowship.

Fatigue frequently accompanies depression and other psychiatric illnesses. In addition, drowsiness is an untoward side effect of some of the medications that are used to treat these disorders. Therefore, even though disciples with psychiatric problems should be dissuaded from missing church and fellowship activities, some special modifications may need to be made. Help them plan their activities in such a way as to take this "fatigue factor" into account. They may not be able to maintain a full schedule for a while (especially if they have been hospitalized), so help them make wise decisions, particularly when it comes to optional activities. If a service is missed for some reason, provide the disciple with notes or a tape of the sermon and encourage him or her to have daily contact with another disciple. Arranging for them to spend time with another Christian who has faced depression and has emerged from it successfully will often give them hope when they are finding it hard to believe things can get better.

Differentiating Between Symptoms and Sin

One of the by-products of being in therapy of any kind (even if the therapist is a disciple) is the tendency to overemphasize feelings and emotions. Unfortunately, it is impossible to treat an emotional disorder without intense self-focus and analysis of feelings.

As disciples, we know that we have to hold to God's standard for our lives and not let our feelings dictate what we do. However, when someone is dealing with a serious emotional disturbance, feelings literally take over and become overwhelming. Disciples dealing with these intense emotions need even more help than usual to differentiate between sin and the expected symptoms of a psychiatric disorder.

For example, people who have experienced some kind of abuse often feel overwhelming anger at themselves as well as their abuser. When these victims become Christians, they have to make a decision to deal with the sin of hatred and forgive the abuser. However, the feelings of anger still persist. Many Christians will either deny feeling angry (which usually makes their depression worse) or question their own conversion because these feelings did not automatically go away at the time of baptism.

Anger is a natural consequence of abuse. The feeling of anger is, in itself, not sinful. In fact, the Bible says that God himself has "burned with anger" over mistreatment of his children. It is the response to anger that is sinful: hatred, resentment, selfishness and lack of forgiveness. In Ephesians 4:26 God tells us that we can feel angry without being led into this sin. Therefore, we need to help disciples *work through* their feelings rather than deny or avoid them. This takes time, patience, effort and prayer.

As noted previously, a person in psychiatric treatment must go through a time of intense self-analysis. During this time the disciple needs to consistently be brought back to the Scriptures in order to diffuse the tendency to become selfish. Remind the person that he or she is a Christian first and foremost and must therefore continue to reach out to others, even during this period of healing and even if that outreach has to be more limited. Allow the person to talk to one or two other disciples about his or her treatment, but at the same time, help the person find ways to serve others, possibly others who are in similar situations. Not only will this help the disciple stay spiritually strong and selfless, but it will also help the disciple combat the low self-esteem and feelings of uselessness that usually accompany depression and most other psychiatric problems.

As Christian psychologists, we are often asked whether or not it is wise to confront a disciple about sin while that person is struggling with an emotional problem. The answer is almost always yes, although this must certainly be done with tact and wisdom. We do not help each other, even disciples who are facing emotional challenges, by overlooking sin. Anything that hurts a person spiritually will also hurt them emotionally and psychologically. In other words, sin is still sin, regardless of one's circumstances. It was this very conviction that prevented Job in the beginning from "charging God with wrongdoing" despite his trials and physical illnesses (Job 1:22).

It is interesting that certain psychiatric conditions tend to predispose people to certain kinds of sin. People with bipolar disorder, for example, must struggle harder to fight against debauchery and loss of self-control. Likewise, people who suffer from depression must combat irritability, fits of rage and the desire to self-medicate with alcohol or drugs. However, patients must be reminded that the psychiatric disorder does not make the sin inevitable, any more than "normal" feelings of loneliness make sexual immorality inevitable, or hurt feelings make hatred acceptable.

Many leaders are hesitant to confront disciples with psychiatric problems out of fear that such confrontation will push the person over the edge. This is a valid concern only if the person is actively suicidal or psychotic. Such disciples must have their immediate needs met first, such as being placed in a safe, supervised environment. The sin can then be dealt with once the crisis has passed. Otherwise, the rule of thumb is to confront sin as you would with any other person who has, through baptism and confession of faith, agreed to live by God's word rather than feelings, circumstances or emotions. Just keep in mind that people with certain emotional illnesses are more likely to accept that they are sinners than to accept the truths about grace and forgiveness.

Be Encouraging

As mentioned earlier, profound feelings of hopelessness and failure accompany most psychiatric disorders, especially depression. A depressed person who is suffering both physically and emotionally will find it hard to believe that he or she will ever feel differently. Therefore, one of the first steps in therapy is to instill hope in the patient. As disciples, we are especially blessed because we have the promises of God to turn to during difficult times. These include promises for healing (for example, Psalm 103:2-5 and 104:3); promises that we have been chosen by God (Ephesians 1:3-14); and the promise that everything will work out for our spiritual good (Romans 8:28). Disciples facing emotional challenges need to be reminded that these promises still apply to them, even when they feel despondent or unworthy. This can be accomplished by having them write down some of God's specific promises, to be read every day and memorized. The very act of doing so will help the disciple to develop an undying belief in God's promises.

Life-Giving Accountability

It is most important to encourage disciples to adhere faithfully to whatever treatment has been prescribed. Pray with them that they will find the right professionals to help them, and then pray for those professionals on the disciples' behalf. Disciples with emotional problems need to be encouraged to follow the recommendations of their doctors and therapists, as long as they are not asked to do anything that is against God's word. Your support of their treatment can help them benefit from that treatment as well as stay faithful to the kingdom.

9

Special Situations: More Advice for Leaders and Friends

There are a few situations that may require special attention when someone is being treated for a psychiatric problem. Should one of these situations occur with someone you are responsible for, be sure to seek lots of advice and pray constantly for wisdom and for God's intervention. *When it comes to dealing with Christians who are facing emotional challenges, we must learn how to rely on God rather than our own knowledge, training or opinions.*

Suicidal Thinking

Suicidal thoughts are very common in people who are severely depressed or psychotic. In fact, this is such a common symptom that many disorders are classified by the additional descriptor "with or without suicidal ideation." Some people erroneously believe that a "true" Christian would never suffer from or struggle with suicidal thoughts. However, the Bible actually documents several instances in which strong, spiritual leaders became so despondent as to express the desire to die. Consider, for example, Elijah, who sat down under a broom tree and prayed to die after fleeing from Jezebel (1 Kings 19:3-4). Or how about Jonah, who after finally getting up the nerve to rebuke the Ninevites, stubbornly sat in the blazing sun because he felt that "it would be better for me to die than to live" (Jonah 4:5-9). Paul says that he "despaired even of life itself" and in his heart "felt the sentence of death" (2 Corinthians 1:8-9). It is clear that Satan will use such thoughts against a Christian during times of distress or depression, just as he uses them to torment people in the world.

Many times we have had disciples confess suicidal thoughts in therapy, only after struggling with those thoughts for days, months or years without letting anyone know. They are usually ashamed to talk about suicidal thoughts because they know that such thoughts are "wrong." However, in the eyes of God, suicidal thoughts are no more sinful than lustful thoughts, impure thoughts, vengeful thoughts, etc. Therefore, if someone you are discipling confesses having suicidal thoughts, make it easy for that person to confess those thoughts without feeling ashamed or embarrassed. In therapy we often ask Christians to talk specifically about their suicidal thoughts so that they can be dealt with directly.

When we are working with Christians who are struggling with suicidal thoughts, we tell them two things: First, that these thoughts are Satan's attempt to get them to give up the fight and lose their salvation (not just their lives) during this very difficult time. The easiest way for Satan to steal away a brother or sister is to convince that person that he or she will never get better and that death is the only way out of a life of suffering. This line of reasoning seems logical to a depressed person. However, the disciple needs help in exposing these as Satan's lies.

The second point that we make is that suicidal thinking is a common, expected symptom of many psychiatric disorders, such as major depression. Christians often feel that they are in sin just by virtue of having these thoughts, even though they perceive them as completely uncontrollable. Therefore, it is helpful to show the disciple that these thoughts are just a form of temptation. Just as alcoholics are tempted to drink, and just as individuals with a history of immorality are tempted to engage in sexual sin, people suffering from depression are tempted to commit suicide. Help the disciple confess at the temptation level and remind him or her that it remains only a temptation unless it is acted upon. Like other temptations, this one can be resisted with the help of God. No matter how strong the temptation, God will provide a way out (1 Corinthians 10:13).

It is troubling that we have counseled some disciples who do not believe that suicide is actually against God's law. If this is the case with your friend, you may need to study with him or her the scriptures about murder and God's authority over life and death. Scriptures such as Jeremiah 10:23, 1 Corinthians 6:19-20 and the last three chapters of Job may be most useful in helping a disciple come to conviction about the sin of suicide. Do not be afraid to confront suicidal thoughts with Scripture!

Hospitalization

The symptoms of a psychiatric disorder sometimes become sufficiently severe to warrant hospitalization. In the past, hospitalization was used quite frequently as a way of intensively treating depression and other emotional problems. However, because of cost concerns, hospitalization is now used only in crisis situations in which someone is considered dangerous to self or others, or when someone requires a high level of medical monitoring and supervision (for stabilization of medications, detoxification, etc.).

Since inpatient psychiatric treatment involves dealing with very sensitive issues, all of the doctors, therapists and employees in psychiatric hospitals are held strictly to the ethic of confidentiality. This means that you will be unable to obtain any information about the patient's progress or treatment without the patient's written permission, regardless of whether you are friend, family, minister or fellow Christian. In fact, written consent must be given by the patient before you will be allowed to have any contact with the patient whatsoever, even by phone. This will force you, as someone who is genuinely concerned about the patient, to trust that God will ultimately work through the facility and the staff to help your brother or sister.

Hospitalization is often just the first step in long-term treatment for an emotional or psychiatric problem. Unfortunately, friends and family tend to think of hospitalization as a cure, and they expect the person to be all better after discharge. This is rarely the case. Patients are released from the hospital only when it has been decided that they are stable enough that their care can be managed safely on an outpatient basis. Even then the patient is usually only in the initial stages of recovery. Do not expect your brother or sister to be back to normal immediately after hospitalization. Instead, the patient will need lots of encouragement to keep up with medication, as well as outpatient appointments with doctors and therapists. We often advise disciples to plan their activities as if they had just had surgery, leaving plenty of time to rest or to ask for help with obligations or duties they may feel unable to perform. Even though the person may look fine on the outside, he or she will still be emotionally and physically fragile following a period in the hospital. Once again, be encouraging, compassionate and supportive—in much the same way as you would with a brother or sister who is recovering from a physical illness.

Finally, it is helpful to know that many of the medicines that are used to treat psychiatric disorders have side effects. The person on an antidepressant, antipsychotic, anxiolytic (antianxiety) or mood-stabilizing medication may tire easily, sleep poorly or have difficulty concentrating. If a person has to discontinue or change medications, he or she may experience even more severe physical symptoms or mood changes. Help the person to modify his or her schedule accordingly and to persevere through these uncomfortable changes.

History of Abuse

Unfortunately, more and more people will become Christians having suffered some kind of physical, sexual or emotional abuse, usually during childhood. It is likely that the disciple will have to deal with many residual difficulties as a result of such cruelty at the hands of others. It is beyond the scope of this book to completely explore the symptoms and problems associated with abuse, and how to help someone who is recovering from an abusive history.[1] However, we can offer a few suggestions that might help if you are discipling someone who has this kind of traumatic past.

People who have suffered abuse in any form, especially long-term abuse, are usually left with a complex array of feelings and behaviors as a result. These difficult feelings or behaviors may be severe and chronic, especially if the abuse occurred in childhood. Symptoms range from chronic depression to anxiety, panic attacks, low self-esteem and other symptoms mentioned previously in our discussion on post-traumatic stress disorder (PTSD). In addition, individuals who grew up in abusive households usually develop inappropriate ways of relating to other people. They may appear aloof, distrustful or extremely oversensitive and "thin-skinned." Those who try to be closest to these people end up bearing the brunt of these emotional and social problems.

Since psychiatric disorders are usually defined by their symptoms, people with long histories of abuse may acquire several diagnoses—including bipolar disorder, PTSD, panic disorder

---

[1]We understand from the editors of DPI that a workbook for those who have been abused in various ways will be appearing in the first part of the year 2000.

and so forth. Do not be frightened if the person you are discipling comes to you with more diagnoses than a medical text. Usually, these diagnoses will have been given by doctors or therapists who were simply trying to describe the complex pattern of behavioral and emotional changes that occur in people who have been abused.

Victims of abuse can change. Those who disciple them can expect to see great changes as God works in the lives of individuals who has suffered from abuse. God detests cruelty and promises that those who abuse will be punished. (See, for example, Exodus 21:22-25, Deuteronomy 22:25-27 and Malachi 2:16.) He is also eager for the restitution of the meek who have had to endure abuse at the hands of others (Psalm 37:7-11).

However, people who have been abused usually struggle with the idea that God loves them and will effect ultimate justice. Such people have difficulty trusting others and understanding God's unconditional love because they have only been exposed to hurtful, imperfect relationships in the world. When young children are abused they often try to make sense of the abuse by blaming themselves or convincing themselves that they have "earned" this punishment in some way. (Although this is incorrect thinking, it helps them feel more powerful and less helpless, as if they could stop the abuse if they could only figure out what they are doing wrong.) Even adults who have made progress in understanding their abusive childhood may still feel very unlovable, inadequate or "damaged."

Therefore, they need help to understand how much God loves them and values them. They need to be reminded that they were made "holy and blameless" at the time of baptism (Ephesians 1:4). However, both the discipler and the disciple need to keep in mind that the emotions of distrust, guilt and self-deprecation will not magically disappear in the baptismal waters. These are issues that the victim of abuse will probably have to face time and again over the course of a lifetime. The best thing that the discipler can do is to listen and then redirect the disciple back to the truths in God's word. Remember, it is God's word—rather than your brilliant and insightful counseling—that truly changes a person. Use the Bible to help the person see that feeling worthless, unloved, distrustful and unforgiving is contrary to the mind and heart of God. Once again it is helpful to see this problem as temptation. The person who has been abused is tempted to believe a lot of untrue things about himself or herself, but that temptation can be resisted with the power of God and the Scriptures.

The Heart of Jesus

Admittedly, it is sometimes difficult for someone who has not suffered a history of abuse to feel compassion for someone who has. The tendency may be to wonder why the person cannot just get over it and move on. If you find it difficult to feel compassion or empathy in this way, take a moment to consider how you would feel if you, or someone you love, had to endure the experience of physical, emotional or sexual abuse. All human beings have been victims of mistreatment at some time (we've been rejected, had our feelings hurt and so forth), but few of us have undergone the kind of cruelty that mental health professionals refer to as "abuse." Before you admonish someone to toughen up and get over it, try to imagine how Jesus would have felt and reacted if he had witnessed a child being abused during his time on the earth. If you can set aside your preconceptions about the so-called "victim mentality" long enough to do that, you will probably be better able to counsel with a compassionate and loving heart.

10

Remaining Faithful Through Emotional Challenges

The previous chapter focused on the responsibility of the discipler or ministry leader in helping Christians who are facing emotional challenges. At the same time, Christians should not be relieved of the responsibility of helping themselves because they have been diagnosed with a psychiatric disorder. Besides seeking appropriate treatment and staying compliant with that treatment, what can you as a Christian do to stay faithful in the face of an emotional illness?

Fortunately, the Bible is replete with examples of great men and women who went through hard times emotionally and had to work to remain faithful to and stay close to God. The most vivid example is David, who left us the legacy of an emotional diary in the book of Psalms. This is why Psalms reads like a roller coaster of moods and feelings, alternating between joyous celebrations of faith and repentance to—sometimes within a few paragraphs—cries of despair, guilt and anguish. David's psalms recount one man's struggle to stay faithful and remain godly in the face of trying circumstances and emotional ups and downs. Although his life remained difficult until his dying day, he remained victorious over his emotional struggles by staying close to God. He summarized this best in Psalm 30:

> Weeping may remain for a night,
>   but rejoicing comes in the morning.
>
> When I felt secure, I said,
>   "I will never be shaken."
> O Lord, when you favored me,
>   you made my mountain stand firm;
> but when you hid your face,
>   I was dismayed.
>
> To you, O Lord, I called;
>   to the Lord I cried for mercy:
> "What gain is there in my destruction,
>   in my going down into the pit?
> Will the dust praise you?
>   Will it proclaim your faithfulness?
> Hear, O Lord, and be merciful to me;
>   O Lord, be my help."
>
> You turned my wailing into dancing;
>   you removed my sackcloth and clothed
>   me with joy,
> that my heart may sing to you and not be silent.
>   O Lord my God, I will give you thanks forever.
>   (Psalm 30:5b-12)

David made it his first priority to stay close to God, and in doing so, he was able to endure everything from persecution to betrayal by friends, marital problems and the deaths of two of his children.

It should be the first priority of every disciple to develop a close, growing, wholehearted relationship with God. This is true regardless of our circumstances or feelings, and whether we are dealing with an emotional disorder or not. As psychologists, we have seen that most Christians who are dealing with psychological problems find it especially difficult to stay close to the Lord. We frequently hear laments such as: "I'm still reading my Bible every day, but I don't get anything out of it anymore"; "Why would God even want to have a relationship with me?"; or "I don't even feel like praying right now." Sound familiar? It is the task of the disciples facing emotional challenges to fight these thoughts and feelings and to expose them for what they are: Satan's attempt to separate them from God. To fight these lies, disciples must focus on the promises they made to God when they became Christians, whether they feel like it or not. To this end, we offer the following recommendations on maintaining a relationship with God.

Faithful in Prayer

Daily prayer is the spiritual nourishment of every Christian. Pray to be healed! David did and was rewarded for his faith (Psalm 30:2). At the same time, pray for the needs of others as a way of staying outwardly focused. It may help to keep a prayer list or journal so that you can see how God is working to make you stronger through your emotional ordeal.

Get real in your prayers and talk to God like you would your best friend. Tell him how bad you feel, what you are afraid of, and what you wish for. Pour out your heart. When you feel unable to pray, use the book of Psalms to call out to God. Make the poems and prayers of Psalms your own, and then use them to speak to God. David and the other writers of Psalms expressed every possible emotion, including:

- depression (Psalms 6:6; 22:1-2; 55:4-7; 77:7-9; 88:3-17)
- abandonment (Psalm 22:1-2)
- fear (Psalms 22:7-16; 56:3-11) and
- hopelessness (Psalm 22:6-7).

In each instance, the author gives voice to his feelings and then refocuses on the blessings and promises of God.

You may want to find a specific psalm that best expresses the way you feel, and then pray through that psalm every day for a time.

Faithful in Bible Study

There is no medication or therapy that is as powerful and effective as God's word. Don't deprive yourself of this component of treatment! Just as a diabetic needs insulin every day, so should you see yourself as equally dependent on a daily dose of Scripture.

One of the biggest obstacles to studying your Bible may be poor concentration. This is a symptom of almost every psychiatric problem we can name. Psychologists can actually see a decrease in intelligence test scores in patients who are acutely depressed, anxious or psychotic. Therefore, your Bible study may need to be adjusted accordingly. You may need to cut down on the time you spend in your Bible and exchange quantity of study for quality. Focus on making your study useful to you, instead of worrying about how many chapters you have read.

We previously mentioned our scripture "prescription cards" that we recommend for disciples in the midst of an emotional crisis. These are index cards with individual verses that can be studied, reviewed and memorized throughout the day. It is better to concentrate on putting one scripture into practice all day than it is to forge through forty-five minutes of reading that you cannot even remember by the time you go to bed! If you are facing an emotional challenge, focus on being faithful with your Bible study, rather than on reading legalistically to assuage your guilt.

The other obstacle to great Bible study may be the tendency to focus only on scriptures that match your mood. Depressed disciples especially seem to have an amazing ability to find (and memorize) every frightening and gloomy verse in the Bible. These scriptures they take as truths set in stone. Yet when confronted with scriptures about God's love and his desire to bless his children (for example, Ephesians 3:16-19, Jeremiah 29:11 and Romans 8:28), they are convinced that these scriptures cannot possibly apply to them!

Therefore, make your Bible study encouraging and uplifting. Wait until later to study Lamentations and Revelation. You can study those out when you feel better. Marinade your mind in hopeful, optimistic scriptures, and use them as godly inoculations against your infections—negative thoughts. Remember, God's words are still true, whether you believe them or not (Isaiah 55:8-9).

Faithful in Fellowship

It may be hard to be around others when you are struggling with a mood disorder, anxiety disorder or thought disorder. It may be hard to keep from focusing on your own overwhelming feelings all the time. In fact on some days it may be hard to just get out of bed and get dressed. However, you still have to fight to stay "healthy" as a Christian. Consider this as one of those warnings you see on the side of a medication bottle: "Failure to meet daily with other Christians will cause certain spiritual decline." This cannot be overstressed.

If you must, get someone to pick you up and take you to church. Sit in the back, if necessary, and get someone to sit with you. If you are in the hospital or temporarily unable to attend, ask for notes, tapes and communion, and arrange a time to be with another Christian. Do whatever it takes, because separation from the body of Christ will cause you to perish, as certainly as a limb will die if it has been amputated from the body. Even when working with non-Christians who are depressed or otherwise emotionally challenged, we recommend physical and social activity as a first line of treatment. Staying in bed and isolating yourself will only make the disorder worse. In fact, many depressed patients have actually ended up hospitalized because they gave in to their vegetative symptoms.

One last word about attending church: Resist the temptation to overpersonalize what you hear in the sermon. People who are depressed or have other emotional problems tend to overanalyze everything because of their feelings of insecurity and inadequacy. Remember that the lessons and sermons that come from the pulpit are meant for the entire church, therefore not every word of correction was meant for you! If something does apply to you, repent, but do not give in to Satan's attempts to make you feel bad about everything you hear. Remember that your feelings are "broken" and cannot be trusted right now. Getting the perspective of a mature disciple will be valuable. So get up, get dressed and go to church, no matter how bad you feel. At the risk of sounding like an ad for aspirin—you'll get better faster and stay stronger spiritually—guaranteed!

Faithful in Discipleship

Discipling relationships are easy when both people are doing great spiritually, physically and emotionally. However, if this were the case all the time, we would not need discipling at all! The fact is, we are all a psychological mess at one time or another, and for this reason we all need help from fellow Christians who are willing to do what needs to be done in order to help us get to heaven. If you suffer from a psychiatric disorder, you are no different from anyone else in this respect. Your problems may be unique to you, but they are not unique to God or even to his church. You still need help to apply and live by God's word. You still need to be rebuked, corrected and—especially—encouraged, even though you may feel as if absolutely no one can understand you because of your situation.

It is Biblical and good, without exception, to seek and follow advice. Most of you will not be discipled by someone with a degree in counseling or psychology. Remember, however, that there is a difference between discipling and therapy. Your discipler is not in your life to treat your disorder; he or she is there to help you apply the Bible to your life. Of course your emotional problems will affect your spiritual growth and consequently, your relationships with those who are discipling you.

You can help your discipling partner tremendously by describing your thoughts and feelings as accurately as possible. In the event that you are being discipled by someone who has not been depressed for more than fifteen minutes out of the last twenty years, you will need to educate that person—with respect and forbearance—on what it feels like to be depressed or anxious. Hopefully, this book will be one that is useful to share with them. By sharing more with them, both of you will grow in knowledge and compassion.

If you are in therapy or taking medication, be sure to keep your discipling partner informed about how your treatment is going. You do not need to repeat every word that was exchanged between you and your therapist, but let your discipler know what issues and recommendations were discussed. In this way your fellow Christian can help with the spiritual aspects of the problem that are not being addressed by the doctor or therapist.

Most importantly, be patient with your leaders and discipling partners. Remember that most people have never had experience helping someone spiritually who is suffering from a psychiatric problem. Consequently, those who are leading you in Christ may feel overwhelmed or incompetent. If this is the case, it may be necessary to seek additional help or advice from someone who has had experience with a similar situation in the past. In any event, fight to keep your relationships strong, and be determined to stay receptive to godly advice.

Faithful in Helping Others

"Come, all you who are thirsty,
    come to the waters;
and you who have no money,
    come, buy and eat!
Come, buy wine and milk
    without money and without cost.
Why spend money on what is not bread,
    and your labor on what does not satisfy?
Listen, listen to me, and eat what is good,
    and your soul will delight in the richest of fare.
Give ear and come to me;
    hear me, that your soul may live.
I will make an everlasting covenant with you,
    my faithful love promised to David.
See, I have made him a witness to the peoples,
    a leader and commander of the peoples.
Surely you will summon nations you know not,
    and nations that do not know you will hasten to
        you,
because of the Lord your God,
    the Holy One of Israel,
    for he has endowed you with splendor."

Seek the Lord while he may be found;
    call on him while he is near.
Let the wicked forsake his way
    and the evil man his thoughts.
Let him turn to the Lord, and he will have mercy on him,
    and to our God, for he will freely pardon.

"For my thoughts are not your thoughts,
    neither are your ways my ways."
declares the Lord. (Isaiah 55:1-8)

Absolutely everyone who has ever struggled with a mental illness has wondered at some point, "Why did God allow this to happen to me?" As noted in our first chapter, disease was one of the natural and godly consequences of man's original disobedience. Like Paul, the thorn in your flesh may serve God's ultimate purpose in some way (2 Corinthians 12:7-10).

Although you may not fully understand that entire purpose until you get to heaven and can ask God personally, you can certainly use your experience to help others in the meantime. Even a short study of gifts and roles in the kingdom will convince you that God intends for each of us to use our particular talents and experiences to strengthen the church (see Romans 12:3-8). This is part of God's amazing plan for his children as individuals and for his kingdom as a whole.

The media constantly reminds us that an alarming number of people in today's society are suffering from mood disorders, thought disorders and problems stemming from trauma or abuse. These numbers seem to be swelling daily. In fact in our clinical work we have come to think of depression as the "emotional cancer" of our time! As God's church grows, all Christians will need to become more and more sensitive to psychiatric challenges and be prepared to help both Christians and non-Christians who are dealing with these problems. If you are a disciple who has managed to stay faithful through a psychiatric illness, you may be uniquely qualified to serve others who are undergoing a similar experience.

Heroes in the Faith

In God's modern-day movement there are many real life examples of Christians who have turned their suffering into a blessing for others. We know of one sister, for instance, who has a long history of abuse, depression and multiple hospitalizations for bipolar disorder. Over the years she has reached out to and helped convert many women with similar backgrounds. Even when she was in the hospital, she never failed to share her faith with other patients and even with the hospital staff. There are also several brothers and sisters who graduated from our Rejoice Always group and then returned to lead smaller groups of their own. We greatly admire these true heroes in the faith who remained faithful through their own struggles and then helped others do the same. Follow their example. You may know more about major depression, generalized anxiety or some other psychiatric disorder than anyone else in your congregation! Find some way to use that knowledge to serve others.

Scriptural 'Prescriptions'

Rx:	*Holy Scripture*
	Disp. q.s.
	Sig. Read everyday p.r.n

(Translation: Read a sufficient amount of Scripture every day, as the need arises.)

Our combined forty years of experience in psychology has led us to one solid conviction about mental health: without God, the most that anyone can possibly hope for—even with the entire arsenal of psychological science available—is survival. No one, mental disorder or not, can have true happiness apart from God. Furthermore, there is no medication in the world—no curative or palliative treatment; no unction, lotion, solution or suspension; no pill, tablet, capsule or injection—that is as powerful as God's word. Non-Christians come to our office day after day seeking help, but if they are closed to God's word, they are depriving themselves of the only true cure! Having to witness this is one of the few downsides of doing what we do for a living.

John 8:31-32 says that if you have made the decision to be a true disciple of Jesus Christ, you can avail yourself of the truth that will set you free—free from sin, free from guilt and free from the hopelessness that plagues people with depression or other psychiatric problems. Studying the Word will help you see that you have a Lord who is concerned about you and can empathize with everything you are going through. As it says in Hebrews:

> For we do not have a high priest who is unable to sympathize with our weaknesses, but we have one who has been tempted in every way, just as we are—yet was without sin. Let us then approach the throne of grace with confidence, so that we may receive mercy and find grace to help us in our time of need. (Hebrews 4:15-16)

So whatever your particular problem is today, there's nothing like a good dose of daily Scripture to cure what ails you! Presented here are some brief Bible studies that we compiled in response to particular issues that arose in our Rejoice Always group. It is our hope that these few short studies will *get you started* in searching out your own "cures" in God's word.

Depression

In the entire Bible there is probably no one who had more reason to be depressed than the godly man Job. This man, who was "blameless and upright," lost everything he had in the course of only a few days as a result of an arbitrary challenge from Satan. Even though he was blameless and did nothing to "earn" his affliction, he was tormented to the point of physical disfigurement (Job 1-2). How did he handle this?

* Look at Job 1:20-22. At first, Job fought against the sin of blaming God for everything that went wrong. This only frustrated Satan, who decided to pour on the pressure even more!

Although Job remained faithful and never charged God with wrongdoing, the pressure took its toll. In Job 10:1-19, Job eventually plummeted into depression. How do we know?

- He hated his life (v1).
- He imagined that God was mad at him (vv3-14).
- He felt guilty (vv15-17).
- He felt worthless and eventually developed what psychiatrists call "passive-suicidal thinking" (vv18-19).

One might think that Job certainly had a right to indulge his depression and give "free rein to [his] complaint." He certainly felt like no one could possibly understand or empathize with his situation, as indicated by his discussions with his friends Bildad, Eliphaz and Zophar. Have you ever felt that way?

As Job eventually found out, physical or emotional struggles are not always the result of personal sin. No one who becomes a disciple is guaranteed an illness-free life. As it says in Romans 8:28, difficult times in the lives of Christians serve God's higher purpose, even though that purpose may not be readily evident at the time. How we handle the struggles— emotional or otherwise—is what counts! So, stay close to God, and do not reject the help of others. Seek the appropriate treatment, but do not give "free rein to [your] complaint" by blaming or second-guessing God. Most of all, do not reject your own life, because there is something great in store for you if you persevere! (Romans 8:18).

Guilt

Read Psalm 38:1-4: Have you ever felt like this? This psalm sounds like a journal entry of someone with major depression. David had plenty to feel guilty about in his life. Interestingly, however, this is one psalm in which his specific sin cannot be identified! He may have just been engaging in what psychologists call "negative introspection," which is the tendency to get extremely self-focused and dwell on all your "bad" characteristics. Why do people do this? Why would people insist on seeing themselves as bad, despite Biblical evidence to the contrary? Although they are contrary to the way God looks at us, feeling bad and feeling guilty serve several purposes:

- They keep life predictable. In a world of emotional ups and downs, sometimes it is just more comfortable staying "down." Feeling guilty is a great way to do that. At least you know what will be in store for you every day!

- They keep life easy. If you convince yourself that you have been (and will always be) a terrible person, then you will never have to put forth the effort to change. If you decide that you are incapable of being a good or happy person, then you will never have to risk disappointment.

- They help you avoid confrontation. Some people have lifelong feelings of guilt as a result of being mistreated or abused by someone, and then being made to feel in some way responsible for that abuse. Consequently, these victims sometimes turn their rage and anger in on themselves (psychologists call this "retroflected" anger) so that they will not have to confront the offending party, especially if that party is someone close to them (like a parent or sibling).

Whatever your reason for feeling guilty, it is contrary to God's intention for you as a disciple. Hebrews 10:19-22 tells us that Jesus absolved us from sin so that we would never have to have a guilty conscience again. No amount of self-punishment or self-deprecation on your part can do that! If you believe in God and the holy Bible, then you must believe that you became his child when you professed your faith, repented and were baptized. Just like a good father, God wants you—his child—to be happy, not guilty.

Here is a challenge: write down ten ways that God has blessed you, proving his love for you. Then go to Ecclesiastes 5:18-20. Realize that God wants you to enjoy these blessings guiltlessly and free of charge, except to remember and appreciate the One from whom those blessings came.

Forgiveness

Some people who have been abused or mistreated struggle with following God's commands to forgive (for example, Colossians 3:12-14). However, forgiveness is what Jesus is all about. Think about the life he led and the type of injustice he suffered as he went to the cross. Then think about his last act before he died.

Read Luke 23:32-34. Having just been beaten, spit on, bullied and tortured, in his last breath Jesus asked God to forgive the very people who tortured him. What was their response after his death? Did they reflect on what he had done and then repent? Most of them did not. This did not matter to Jesus—his wish for their pardon was unconditional. In contrast, most of us are willing to forgive only if those who wrong us apologize or see the error of their ways.

Read 1 John 4:19-21. God gave us the capacity to love and forgive. Then, he *commanded* us to love. Think about why you find it difficult to forgive a certain person. Are you harboring a vengeful attitude: "I'll never forgive him until he has been plagued with guilt, begged my forgiveness and been made to suffer like I have"? Do not worry. God will avenge the wrongs that have been perpetrated against his children (Deuteronomy 32:35, Hebrews 10:30). In the meantime, remind yourself that Jesus made no conditions when he begged for his abusers to be forgiven. God will not grant you peace of heart until you can forgive unconditionally. That's because he wants his forgiveness of us to be reflected in the way we forgive each other. So, pray to be able to forgive, and then do it.

Facing Conflict

People who suffer from depression, PTSD and anxiety disorders usually carry around lots of emotional baggage from the past. In the course of therapy they invest considerable amounts of time and energy trying to deal with hurt feelings from previous relationships. The last thing they need is to allow bitter roots (Hebrews 12:15) to grow in their current relationships with their brothers and sisters in Christ.

Most Christians whom we have seen in therapy have such low self-esteem and are filled with so much self-doubt that they are chronic conflict avoiders. Whenever they start to develop any bad feelings about someone, they instantly decide that those feelings cannot possibly be right, thereby avoiding a confrontation. Or, they decide that they will be seen as a whiner or a complainer if they voice their attitude about someone. In reality they are just too afraid to deal directly with the issue.

Look at Ephesians 4:22-27. Paul taught how to deal with our resentments toward others in a righteous way. He said that in doing so we must set aside our "deceitful desires," including the desire to withdraw, keep our feelings to ourselves and nurse our resentments. Jesus commanded us to deal with conflict (Matthew 18:15-17), because to not do so breeds disunity. In Ephesians 4:31 Paul admonished us to "get rid of all bitterness," because this is best for our mental as well as spiritual health.

Therefore, if you harbor resentments toward a brother or sister, stop avoiding conflict. Do not worry about who is right and who is wrong, and stop wondering if the situation is even worth addressing. If an issue is making you more depressed or angry, then it has to be dealt with, no matter what. All conflicts in God's kingdom can be dealt with righteously if we are each trying to practice the love and forgiveness of Christ.

Self-Concept

Look at Psalm 139:13-16. It has been our experience that Christians who are facing psychiatric problems each have an abysmal self-concept. Why? Because in addition to the normal demands and expectations of the world, they also have the pressure of trying to be like Jesus. Instead of seeing themselves as "wonderfully made," as the psalm says, they just consider themselves "a piece of work." They perceive themselves as especially flawed because they have a psychiatric problem.

Read 2 Corinthians 12:7-10. Paul, too, was "flawed." Some hypothesize that he had some kind of problem with his eyes, but who really knows what his "thorn" was? It may very well have been depression or some other psychiatric illness. Whatever it was, Paul delighted in his weakness, and even bragged about it, because it constantly forced him to stay humble and to rely on God.

Look at Isaiah 45:9-12: What is God saying here? He reminds us that we are each but a "potsherd among the potsherds" to help us keep things in perspective. We are not his equals, and we are to be completely reliant on him. However, if you think of yourself as damaged or defective, you are insulting the very work of the Maker. The Creator of the universe chose to make you to his own specifications, for his own purpose.

Your challenge is to see your emotional problem as an opportunity. An episode of depression or anxiety may be God's way of softening your heart and giving you the opportunity to call on his power. Or, like the Gerasene demoniac, you may be one through whom God has chosen to display his power by affecting a complete cure. Do not forget that you are "fearfully and wonderfully made"!

Anxiety

Anxiety is a feeling and a physical state that stems from what we think. Some people worry about things so much that it becomes a habit, making them anxious most of the time. What are some of the things you worry about the most? List five of them, then read Matthew 6:25-34. Jesus' injunctions here are easier said than done. Of all the commands that Jesus gave while he was on earth, some people find this the most difficult to follow. However, this scripture clearly turns worry into a form of disobedience. It is sinful to worry. Fortunately, Philippians 4:4-9 gives us a three-step prescription to stop anxiety.

Step 1: STOP!

Verse 6 tells us not to be anxious about anything. Stop anxious thoughts by identifying them and confronting them as they happen! What do you feel like and act like when you are becoming anxious? What are you thinking about? Teach yourself to interrupt the process by saying to yourself, "I'm worrying" or "I'm being anxious."

Step 2: DROP!

As soon as you catch yourself worrying or feeling anxious, drop to your knees and pray. Tell God what you are feeling and/or fearing. Then ask him for what you want or need. Be specific!

Step 3: ROLL!

Verse 8 says "whatever is true, whatever is noble, whatever is right, whatever is pure, whatever is lovely, whatever is admirable—if anything is excellent or praiseworthy—think about such things." Replace your anxious thoughts with a "roll" of positive, thankful thoughts. Make a list of all the things for which you are thankful, all the great things God has done in your life and all the miracles you hope to see. Keep a copy of this roll in your car, your Bible or your desk at work. Rehearse it repeatedly until you can run through it by memory. In this way you will inoculate yourself against anxiety by replacing your mental "worry tape" with your "thankful tape." Then, "the peace of God, which transcends all understanding, will guard your hearts and your minds in Christ Jesus" (Philippians 4:7).

Suicide

It is amazing to think that most of the men and women in the Bible were just typical people who were allowed to take some part in God's ultimate plan. They were not superheroes who were immune to physical or emotional pain. In fact, there are many stories of men who were so depressed or plagued with guilt that they eventually contemplated taking their own lives—some actually did. However, suicide in the Bible is always associated with unrighteousness and evil. See, for example, the stories of:

- Zimri (1 Kings 16:15-19), who led a rebellion and killed himself after being king for only seven days.
- Saul (1 Chronicles 10:1-14)—his suicide was a final act of cowardice that served as retribution for consulting a medium rather than relying on the Lord.
- Judas (Matthew 27:1-5), could not live with his own guilt, and decided to take his life rather than repent of his sin.

In contrast, there were also righteous men who contemplated suicide, just as many do at one time or another, but refused to submit to that temptation. Consider, for example:

- Moses (Numbers 11:10-15), who asked God to put him to death because he felt incapable of meeting the needs of everyone who was put in his care.
- Elijah (1 Kings 19:1-5), who also asked to die after being persecuted for taking a stand against paganism.
- Jonah (Jonah 1:1-16), who tried to have himself killed when he saw that his presence on the ship was endangering others.
- Job (Job 3), who preferred to die perhaps rather than blaspheme by blaming God for his troubles.

As you can see, it was only those with unrighteous motives who completed the act of taking their own lives.

God, and only God, is in charge of life and death (Deuteronomy 32:39, 1 Samuel 2:6). He determines the exact times, places and circumstances for every man and woman, for the sole purpose of putting each one of us in a position to have a relationship with him (Acts 17:26-28). We need to be very grateful for his plans for us.

No one knows how his or her own "book" is going to end. Of one thing you can be sure, though—God has great plans for those who persevere and remain in him. The miseries of this world will blow away like chaff in the wind when we finally see his face and avail ourselves of his promises. As it says in Jeremiah 29:11-13:

"For I know the plans I have for you," declares the Lord, "plans to prosper you and not to harm you, plans to give you hope and a future. Then you will call upon me and come and pray to me, and I will listen to you. You will seek me and find me when you seek me with all your heart."

Who Are We?

Discipleship Publications International (DPI) began publishing in 1993. We are a nonprofit Christian publisher affiliated with the International Churches of Christ, committed to publishing and distributing materials that honor God, lift up Jesus Christ and show how his message practically applies to all areas of life. We have a deep conviction that no one changes life like Jesus and that the implementation of his teaching will revolutionize any life, any marriage, any family and any singles household.

Since our beginning we have published more than 75 titles; plus we have produced a number of important, spiritual audio products. More than one million volumes have been printed, and our works have been translated into more than a dozen languages—international is not just a part of our name! Our books are shipped regularly to every inhabited continent.

To see a more detailed description of our works, find us on the World Wide Web at www.dpibooks.com. You can order books by calling 1-888-DPI-BOOK twenty-four hours a day. From outside the US, call 781-937-3883, ext. 231 during Boston-area business hours.

We appreciate the hundreds of comments we have received from readers. We would love to hear from you. Here are other ways to get in touch:

Mail: DPI, One Merrill St., Woburn, MA 01801
E-mail: dpibooks@icoc.org

Find us on the World Wide Web

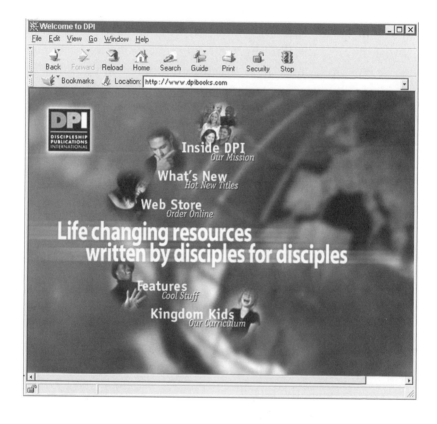

www.dpibooks.com
1-888-DPI-BOOK
outside US: 781-937-3883 x231